it starts with a dream

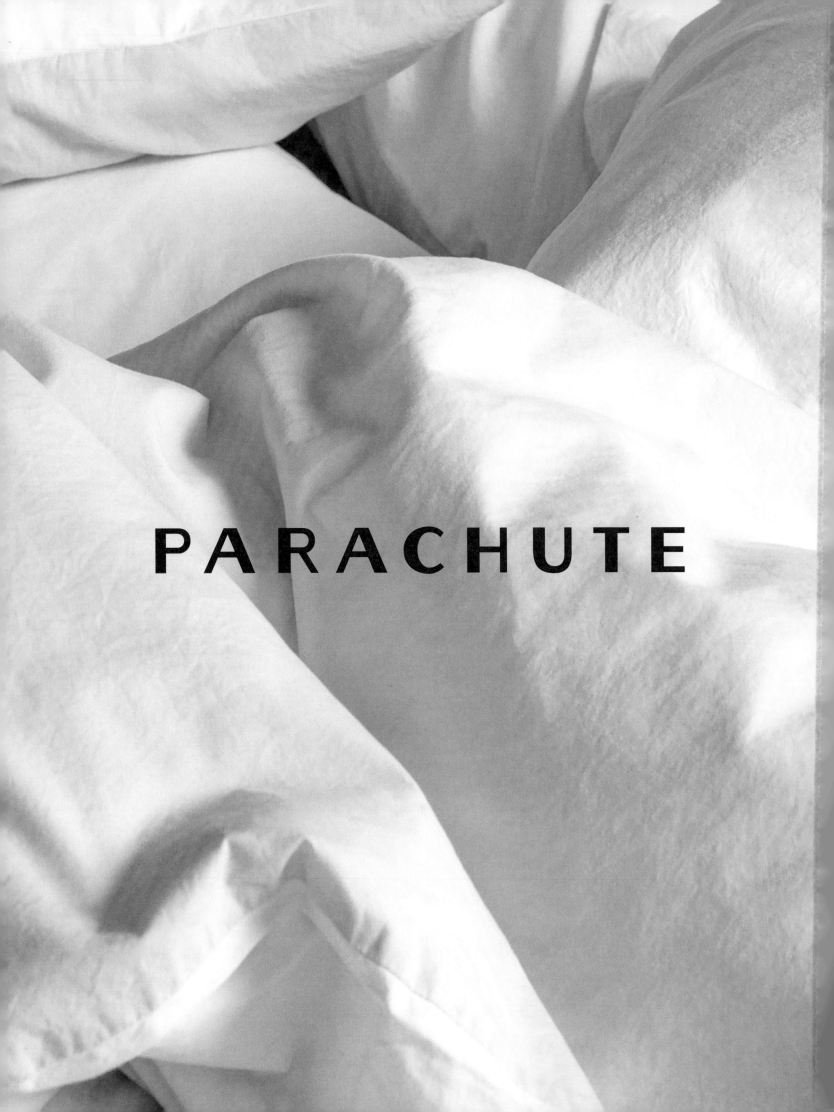

Thoughtfully designed everyday essentials.

FEW THINGS NEVER CHANGE

WE CELEBRATE THE ULTIMATE CHAIR.

THE WAY IT IS. THE WAY FINN JUHL INTENDED IT.

NO GLITTERING ANNIVERSARY EDITION.

WHY CHANGE AN ORIGINAL?

HOUSE OF FINN JUHL

finnjuhl.com

70TH ANNIVERSARY
THE CHIEFTAIN CHAIR

HFJ

LINDBERG

KINFOLK

FOUNDER & CREATIVE DIRECTOR
Nathan Williams

EDITOR-IN-CHIEF
John Clifford Burns

EDITOR
Harriet Fitch Little

ART DIRECTOR - PRINT
Christian Møller Andersen

DESIGN DIRECTOR
Alex Hunting

BRAND DIRECTOR
Amy Woodroffe

DESIGNER & ART DIRECTOR
Staffan Sundström

COPY EDITOR
Rachel Holzman

COMMUNICATIONS DIRECTOR
Jessica Gray

PRODUCER
Cecilie Jegsen

STUDIO MANAGER
Susanne Buch Petersen

**SALES & DISTRIBUTION
DIRECTOR**
Edward Mannering

**BUSINESS OPERATIONS
MANAGER**
Kasper Schademan

EDITORIAL ASSISTANTS
Natalia Lauritzen
Gabriele Dellisanti

CONTRIBUTING EDITORS
Michael Anastassiades
Jonas Bjerre-Poulsen
Andrea Codrington Lippke
Ilse Crawford
Margot Henderson
Leonard Koren
Hans Ulrich Obrist
Amy Sall
Matt Willey

WORDS
Precious Adesina
Alex Anderson
Rima Sabina Aouf
Ellie Violet Bramley
Katie Calautti
Stephanie D'Arc Taylor
Djassi DaCosta Johnson
Cody Delistraty
Gabriele Dellisanti
Daphnée Denis
Bella Gladman
Tim Hornyak
Robert Ito
Kyla Marshell
Sean Michaels
Megan Nolan
Debika Ray
Blythe Roberson
Asher Ross
Laura Rysman
Rhian Sasseen
Neda Semnani
Charles Shafaieh
Ben Shattuck
Pip Usher
Annick Weber

CROSSWORD
Anna Gundlach

PUBLICATION DESIGN
Alex Hunting Studio

PHOTOGRAPHY
Gustav Almestål
Daniel Asater
Ted Belton
Luc Braquet
Rala Choi
Justin Chung
Luc Coiffait
Claire Cottrell
Pascale Georgiev
Marsy Hild Thorsdottir
Dima Hohlov
Lino Lago
Lindsay Lange
Romain Laprade
Emman Montalvan
Linus Morales
Christian Møller Andersen
Aaron Tilley
Zoltan Tombor

STYLING, HAIR & MAKEUP
Marina Andersson
Jesse Arifien
Matilda Beckman
Jermaine Daley
Taan Doan
Lisa Jahovic
Jacob Kajrup
Patricia Lagmay
Cyril Laine
Pernilla Löfberg
Josephine Mai
Sandy Suffield
Camille-Joséphine Teisseire
Nicole Wittman
Alana Wright

COVER PHOTOGRAPH
Romain Laprade

ISSUE 33
Kinfolk (ISSN 2596-6154) is published quarterly by Ouur ApS, Amagertorv 14, 1, 1160 Copenhagen, Denmark. Printed by Taylor Bloxham Limited in Leicester, United Kingdom. Color reproduction by PH Media in Roche, United Kingdom. All rights reserved. No part of this publication may be reproduced, distributed or transmitted in any form or by any means, including photocopying or other electronic or mechanical methods, without prior written permission of the editor-in-chief, except in the case of brief quotations embodied in critical reviews and certain other noncommercial uses permitted by copyright law. The US annual subscription price is $87 USD. Airfreight and mailing in the USA by Worldnet Shipping Inc., 156-15, 146th Avenue, 2nd Floor, Jamaica, NY 11434, USA. Application to mail at periodicals postage prices is pending at Jamaica NY 11431. US Postmaster: send address changes to Kinfolk, Worldnet Shipping Inc., 156-15, 146th Avenue, 2nd Floor, Jamaica, NY 11434, USA. Subscription records are maintained at Ouur ApS, Amagertorv 14, 1, 1160 Copenhagen, Denmark.

info@kinfolk.com
www.kinfolk.com

Published by Ouur Media
Amagertorv 14, Level 1
1160 Copenhagen, Denmark

The views expressed in Kinfolk magazine are those of the respective contributors and are not necessarily shared by the company or its staff.

SUBSCRIBE
Kinfolk is published four times a year. To subscribe, visit kinfolk.com/subscribe or email us at *info@kinfolk.com*

CONTACT US
If you have questions or comments, please write to us at *info@kinfolk.com*. For advertising inquiries, get in touch at *advertising@kinfolk.com*

TF Design
Modern Designs in Resin

tf.design

tf

Welcome

Perhaps you don't need educating on the state of education: You've seen in the news that the best colleges can be bribed, or that for-profit institutions have become debt factories for those who attend. Power should not equal knowledge, but the financial burden of higher education often makes it so. Meanwhile, students who do make it to college are under pressure to approach "book learning" with a tunnel vision that steamrolls more creative ways of thinking. This issue of *Kinfolk* rejects the definition of a good education as one that ends with good grades.

In putting together our fall issue, we considered education as a lifelong pursuit: What can we learn about our bodies, minds, beliefs and societies, and who can teach us? In Los Angeles, we meet Erica Chidi Cohen, the co-founder of Loom—specializing in schooling its (adult) students on bodies, healthcare and better sex. For Chidi Cohen, this new pedagogy is a response to political failures. "If we can't get people healthcare, we need to get them education," she says.

However, a desire to think beyond traditional schools doesn't preclude the urge to improve them. On page 164 we go to work with Liz Kleinrock, an elementary school teacher making waves with her incisive approach to teaching kids about "taboo" topics. Her philosophy of education is future-focused: "How can we make kids better than us?"

The people we meet in Issue Thirty-Three prove just how many different paths can lead to a meaningful career. Montreal-based producer Kaytranada found success so early that he never finished high school, whereas Belgian painter Michaël Borremans spent a decade working as a teacher prior to becoming an acclaimed figurative artist. And some people manage to sidestep the idea of a "calling" altogether: Waris Ahluwalia has funneled his bonhomie into being an actor, model, jewelry designer and activist. Kyla Marshell chronicles his many marvelous lives on page 42.

Our essay writers chew over big topics—like what it means to hit "rock bottom," and how to confront climate anxiety—but also small conundrums: Turn to page 182 to explore the limits of extreme animal grooming. Elsewhere there are bubbles, puzzles and a fashion editorial that takes the form of an all-night party. As Waris Ahluwalia reminds us: "We're all dying. But if we can do it while we're dancing?"

JOHN CLIFFORD BURNS & HARRIET FITCH LITTLE

"The outside world gets confused unless you have a role to play."
WARIS AHLUWALIA – P. 42

Photograph: Zoltan Tombor

PART THREE

Education

"It's not just about knowing something, it's about understanding it."
CHRISTINE DODDINGTON – P. 141

PART FOUR

Directory

Photograph: Romain Laprade

ERIK
jørgensen

WWW.ERIK-JOERGENSEN.COM

OVO DESIGNER DAMIAN WILLIAMSON

Ovo is a refined easy chair, designed by Damian Williamson, with striking curves resting on a rigid squared steel frame. The same steel is also used as a beautiful slim line connecting the back and the front of the chair. As a result, you achieve a playful integration between the leather and the steel while hiding the stitched seam at the same time.

The Ovo design is first and foremost about generosity but also great comfort. The chair is welcoming and very comfortable to sit in - it invites you to sit back and relax. Whether you place it in the comfort of your own private home, a relaxing hotel suite or a lobby, it will be the perfect fit.

marset

Taking care of light

1

Starters

RIMA SABINA AOUF

Against Rock Bottom

There is always further to fall.

Few places suck readers in like a rock bottom. The media is full of stories of people waking up to find themselves without their job, their home, their family—potentially every marker of security and respect—and then clawing their way back. Why? We are not just voyeurs slowing down at a car crash but storytellers entranced by a strong dramatic arc. We are explorers who want to know what knowledge our fellow travelers have gleaned after crossing the abyss.

But not everyone is enamored with this trope. "The concept of 'rock bottom' should be retired from usage," says Peg O'Connor, author of *Life on the Rocks: Finding Meaning in Addiction and Recovery*. The idea of "hitting bottom" is particularly entrenched in the fields of addiction psychology and treatment, and yet it is a common misperception that anyone with an addiction will need to experience the shock and estrangement of this metaphorical place before they can truly start on the path to recovery.

There are obvious pitfalls to this approach: One is that a person who hasn't lost all these things can live in denial about their circumstances for a long time. Another is that the concept of a rock bottom implies there's nowhere further to fall. "Many people assume there's some objective 'rock bottom' or set of losses or consequences so

severe that someone will have no choice but to quit," says O'Connor. "Unfortunately too many people realize it's untrue far too late."

Part of the problem is that extreme stories reinforce the idea that rock bottom is a binary construct—you either are there or you aren't. For example, people in Alcoholics Anonymous have to admit they are flawed; it's stigmatizing. But current neuroscience is more inclined to support the idea of a spectrum; the biggest influence is not *who* we are but *when* we encounter a substance or activity, and what else is going on in our lives and brains at the time. In the *DSM-5*, the most recent edition of the psychiatrists' handbook, for example, the term "alcoholism" is out and "alcohol-use disorder" is in, with subcategories of mild, moderate and severe.

In her book *Unbroken Brain: A Revolutionary New Way of Understanding Addiction*, the journalist Maia Szalavitz, writing from both expertise and experience, argues that the concept of rock bottom has infected addiction treatment, particularly in the US. Szalavitz calls it a pseudoscience, built up over decades by AA, where it's seen as the catalyst to get people onto the 12 Steps. The concept also echoes through other "tough love" treatment approaches, as well as the punitively inclined justice system; think of the way loved ones

who offer material or emotional support are branded enablers. "If addiction were truly seen as a medical disorder, we'd see it as sick and twisted to try to 'disable' people who have it," says Szalavitz. "If the concept of 'enabling' were accurate, then providing clean needles and prescribing heroin would make people stay addicted forever—in fact, these methods are both linked with faster recovery, not longer addiction."

That's not to guilt people who have had to cut off an addicted family member or friend—sometimes it's the best way to keep yourself, and others in your life, safe. But empathy, support and community are approaches backed up by evidence.

The way forward, minus the detour to the bottom? "If we want to overcome any type of addiction, we need to start looking at why we engage in the behavior," says Szalavitz. "It's usually because of despair, trauma or mental illness. Once you look at and treat the source problem and teach people tools for avoiding relapse, recovery becomes possible."

At a time when conversations about mental health are part of the mainstream, the stories we tell about ourselves and other people matter. The rock bottom trope features in some riveting, instructive and inspiring yarns. But it's not the only tale in the sea.

Stories about hitting rock bottom appeal to us from an early age. Ex-offenders and addicts are often enlisted to deliver cautionary talks to schoolchildren.

STARTERS

Double Square 1999-2000 by Euan Uglow. Courtesy of Marlborough Gallery

Left Photography: Courtesy of Ormaie, Mr Porter and Chanel. Right Photograph: Pascale Georgiev from *An Atlas of Rare & Familiar Color* (Atelier Éditions)

SMELL OF SUCCESS

by Pip Usher

For scent makers, secrecy has long been a key ingredient in their success. Check the product label of a bottle of perfume or a scented candle, and components are often deliberately left vague to throw competitors off the scent. Yet fragrances can include dozens of undisclosed synthetic chemicals, some of which are classified as hazardous. The side effects of such hidden ingredients—including headaches, blotchy skin and reduced sperm count—have inspired a recent push for companies to become more transparent about the ingredients of their scented products. Despite the competitive edge granted by trade secrets, companies are starting to realize that their clandestine habits simply end up smelling fishy. (Top: Papier Carbone by Ormaie Paris. Center: Classic Scent by Claus Porto. Bottom: N°5 Eau de Parfum by Chanel.)

ASHER ROSS

Pinch of Mystery

The bitter truth about secret ingredients.

In the children's book *Strega Nona*, a village herbalist in Calabria owns a magic pot that can produce an endless flow of delicious pasta. Her boarder, a bumbling oaf named Big Anthony, tries to use the pot while she is away, bringing disaster. His mistake? He didn't know to blow three kisses after chanting the magic spell.

Spoken about in whispers, guarded by *baachans*, *bubbies* and *bibis* the world over, culinary secrets—most often ingredients—are handed down with ritualistic seriousness, like cast-iron pans. And yet these secrets often turn out to be quite ordinary: a pinch of pepper in the strawberry pie, a touch of sugar in the ragù, a dash of plum vinegar in the pot roast. And yet we obsess, arguing beyond reason that our family's sweet potato pie is like no other, or rushing to a restaurant to taste the latest in the cult of authenticity. The secret, you see, is that the chef uses these particular *angulas* from Lisbon, or Iranian sumac, or Winesap apples from her family orchard in Connecticut.

All delicious, of course. But it's worth understanding how susceptible we are to the mythos of the secret ingredient, which is exploited eagerly by brands. Coca-Cola has been ostentatiously guarding its recipe for more than a hundred years, storing it in a series of increasingly sophisticated vaults. The formula could easily be synthesized in any modern laboratory and is protected by copyright, not tight lips. But the company knows that the idea of a secret formula transforms its mixture of corn syrup, citric acid and caramel into something ineffable.

Master storytellers have always used the unknown to activate the artistry of their listener's own imagination. Steven Spielberg knew this when he hid the shark for the first half of *Jaws*. And grandpa knew it when he refused to say what went into the turkey brine. We like to believe that food can touch our souls, heal us in heartbreak and bring us into communion with those who came before. And it can. Memory provides part of this magic, chemistry another. But all falls flat without imagination, and the secrets that awaken it. If the telling is right, any secret will do.

ELLIE VIOLET BRAMLEY

A Fine Line

The case for queueing.

For many, "queue" is a byword for tedium; it's time mired in the mundane when you could be out there being your best self. It's a blip in a lunch break, a vacuum in an otherwise fulfilling day.

Our animosity toward lines has been well-researched—as have ways to mitigate it. According to queue psychologists, the answer to making waiting in line less irksome isn't necessarily to minimize the amount of time spent toe-tapping. As "Dr. Queue," the MIT professor Richard Larson, put it to *The New York Times*: "Often the psychology of queuing is more important than the statistics of the wait itself." Research has shown that much of our displeasure comes from the specifics of the experience—from the boredom to any perceived grievances: here's looking at you, line cutters.

Studies have found that lines feel less onerous when they are more interesting. People who have

nothing to do even perceive wait times to be longer than those who are entertained. It might sound obvious, but distractions such as mirrors, TV screens and phones have been shown to do a good job of taking our minds off the wait. Injustice only exacerbates the disdain. Research has shown that one long serpentine line—think a mammoth slog to passport control—is often favored over lots of shorter ones, where someone who joined their queue after you joined yours might still get to the front quicker, adding injustice to the injury of waiting.

Not all lines are created equal, either. Enter what has been coined the "fun queue," or what some have called the modern phenomenon of the "non-mandatory line": the wait for much-hyped streetwear to drop, to get into Wimbledon, for long-anticipated installments in book or film series, or to get into a buzzy new restaurant.

Waiting in these cases will likely build excitement rather than dull it. Or perhaps it becomes part of the experience, an event in itself and a place to congregate with people who share your interests. This is something that theme parks have mastered—at Disneyland, the queue is seen as part of the ride. Turn it into enough of an event and people will forget what they're lining up for and start to enjoy themselves instead.

But even the most mundane queues have overlooked virtues. It doesn't have to be the chaff of life while you wait to get to the good stuff. If we know how long we have to wait, we'll settle in—studies have shown that uncertainty intensifies queue-stress. Then maybe we can reframe even the dullest of lines— to pay for your lunchtime sandwich—as an opportunity. It's a moment of stillness in an otherwise frenetic day, to let your mind wander, just for a bit.

VANITY FAIRS

by Pip Usher

When the German Pavilion was erected at the 1929 Barcelona International Exhibition, it served one purpose: To "[give] voice to the spirit of a new era." Designed by architect Ludwig Mies van der Rohe—a man legendary enough to be known simply as "Mies"—and Lilly Reich, the pavilion was built to show the world what the democratically elected and progressively minded postwar Weimar Republic was all about. The resulting structure has been celebrated as one of Mies' most daring works. Focused on the concept of free-flowing space, the pavilion featured a fluid interior with slabs of polished marble and glass that acted as walls. A flat roof appeared to float above, supported by slender steel columns. Outside, a large rectangular pool was filled with smooth stones that gleamed in the water. Despite its beauty, the pavilion was disassembled once the fair finished. How could such a building—one that was later lauded as a seminal piece of modernist architecture—survive for only a few months? Therein lies the peculiarity of a pavilion. They exist as grand architectural gestures designed to serve no purpose other than to impress and inspire. Those footing the bill for their construction must hope that they leave a lasting impact on visitors in very little time. Decades later, Mies would coin the phrase "less is more" to describe his aesthetic, and the pavilion was eventually reconstructed in Barcelona. The pavilion's stark design captures Mies' devotion to minimalism—but it's raison d'être remains decidedly extravagant. *Photography by Lindsay Lange*

The self-possessed singer on the importance of vulnerability.

Michael Kiwanuka

When Michael Kiwanuka decided to pursue music professionally, he thought that would mean becoming a teacher or a session musician. Instead, the British artist has released two albums and been nominated for a Mercury Prize twice. Listening to his songs, it is clear why so many people identify with the music of this unassuming 32-year-old: There is a sense of honesty and passion in every soaring note. For Kiwanuka, however, creating music is about more than just the final product. It's about "being true to who you are," he says. It's also about sharing with his audience in a way that goes deeper than albums and Instagram posts, which is why he released the short documentary *Out Loud!* last year, giving a glimpse into his life on tour and in live performances. "I just wanted to show people what I do in a creative and artistic way," he explains.

PA: *You wrote the title track for the TV show* Big Little Lies *and appeared on the soundtrack of* The Get Down. *Do you think your music lends itself particularly well to TV?* **MK:** I think my music works for a television or movie scene because I'm trying to evoke another place or dimension. I like cinematic styles of music and I'm always trying to make it sound like that, even if it's not intended for TV.

PA: *Your song "Black Man in a White World" is about the shyness you felt growing up as a result of not*

fitting in. Have you now found confidence in yourself? **MK:** I now feel comfortable being different and it's something I embrace and enjoy. I realize that's a common trait for creative people. You're making your own world so you're always going to feel a little detached or misunderstood.

PA: *Romantic love plays such a formative role for many musicians. Around the time of your debut, you said you'd never been in love. Is that still true?* **MK:** I've been married for three years so it's definitely not true now. Even then, there was no absence of it. The song "I'll Never Love" was more about love going wrong. The absence of love brings out emotions that I like in music, the melancholy side, though the presence of it is more enjoyable. Both emotions are definitely conducive to great songs and art. However, I do find it easier to make sad music.

PA: *Vulnerability was a key theme on* Love & Hate. *Why?* **MK:** People trust you more and connect with you better if you let your guard down and show your real side. It's the same with music. If you're hiding things, it's difficult for people to connect.

PA: *Earlier this year you appeared on Little Simz's album. The song "Flowers" was very much a mixture of both of your styles of music. Was this intentional?* **MK:** Yes. In good collaborations, the two artists are able to express themselves the way they are. Inflo produced my

Photography: Luc Coiffait

Kiwanuka was catapulted into the spotlight when he won the BBC Sound of 2012 award ahead of Frank Ocean and Azealia Banks.

album *Love & Hate*, but also Little Simz's *Grey Area* album. There was a nice link there so we all felt comfortable with each other and were able to do our thing. I felt blessed to lend my voice to it.

PA: *Would you be interested in incorporating more genres into your work?* **MK:** I've always wanted to collaborate with many genres. The more comfortable I am as a singer, the more fun collaborating is as there are less insecurities and I throw a bit more caution to the wind. There are so many great young British artists.

PA: *You once said, "It's important to have views, not to be everybody's best friend," referring to musicians using their fame to shed light on serious issues. What's on your mind?*

MK: There's so much happening around the world but I do have issues close to my heart. I'm a part of Kids Club Kampala, which helps orphans in the slums of Kampala [Uganda], giving them homes, clothes, schooling. Also, there are abandoned kids here in the UK. There are a lot of people without parents and loving families. These are things we can't take for granted.

PA: *There was a large gap between your two albums, and now a considerable amount of time has passed again. What can we expect next?* **MK:** This next album is a lot more vivid and a bit more experimental and abstract at times, but then there's still the same soulfulness and emotion. That's as much as I can say without playing it.

ALEX ANDERSON

Word: Skeuomorph

Afraid of change? Make new things look like old ones.

Etymology: Henry Colley March, a British physician and amateur archaeologist, devised the word in 1889 by combining the Greek *skeuos*, which means container or implement, with *morphē*, a reference to shape.

Meaning: In an age deeply preoccupied with ornament, March offered a handy term for a common but often awkwardly described kind of decoration. "The forms demonstrably due to structure require a name," he wrote. "If those taken from animals are called zoomorphs and those taken from plants phyllomorphs, it will be convenient to call those derived from structure skeuomorphs." The lion foot at the base of a chair leg is a zoomorph, and a foliated wrought iron gate is a phyllomorph. But a skeuomorph? In archaeology, the word refers to an inherent or functional aspect of an older object that has survived as an ornament in a newer version—a basket pattern on a ceramic container, or carpentry details on a stone temple.

Skeuomorphs are still ubiquitous. The flickering of an LED candle flame, the digital speedometer dial on a new car's dashboard, the variegated swirls of plastic tortoiseshell glasses, the shutter click of a phone camera—all skeuomorphs, all ornamental manifestations of what was unavoidably present in an earlier version. As with most design choices, these anachronisms can generate controversy. What may seem disturbingly fake to some is comfortingly retro for others. Anthropologist John H. Blitz points out that "encounters with unfamiliar innovations trigger different emotional responses… some people may not want the same old objects, but others do not wish to relinquish the associated positive emotions… skeuomorphs are part of the social process that resolves this innovation dilemma." They can make new technologies reassuringly familiar, even if their appearance seems gratuitously decorative.

The role of skeuomorphs played out vividly in 2013 when Apple flattened parts of its phone and computer interfaces. Suddenly the word entered everyday conversation just as some familiar skeuomorphs disappeared—3D buttons became colored circles, the notepad app no longer looked like a pad of paper, and reading an e-book didn't require flipping over digital pages anymore.

John Brownlee, an editor for Cult of Mac, sneered at these "tacky design crimes" and was happy to see them go, but not everyone agreed. Gizmodo's Kelsey Campbell-Dollaghan countered that "skeuomorphism is not a design crime. It marks the settling of new technological frontiers."- Clearly, these functional ornaments can outlast their usefulness but skeuomorphs often conveniently hint at what new tools have to offer.

Computer interface designers use skeuomorphs liberally. The floppy disk "save" symbol and clipboard "paste" button are both examples.

Photograph: Aaron Tilley, Styling: Sandy Suffield

Artwork: Fake Abstract (On J. K. Stieler) by Lino Lago

RHIAN SASSEEN

How to say goodbye for good.

See You Never

"Plan an appropriate time to talk before the departure," recommends one web page entitled "How to Say Goodbye." The cartoons that accompany it are as stilted and formulaic as each piece of advice. "Talk about all the good times you've had," it urges. "When it's time to leave, make it brief and sincere." Implicit in its offerings: To say goodbye can be painful or terrifying. Absence, even necessary absence, can create guilt, and yet, it's also essential in order to experience the world. "That's why I went," says one character in Susan Sontag's *Unguided Tour*: "To say goodbye. Whenever I travel, it's always to say goodbye."

A wave, a bow, a block on the phone. There are different ways of saying goodbye. Some are necessarily worse than others: a lover's farewell, a lover's death. Then there are the mundane varieties: goodbye to co-workers, classmates, cities and apartments. You cannot move forward without saying goodbye. Pop culture says so, high culture says so. It's Shakespeare's "sweet sorrow," it's Joan Didion's "goodbye to all that."

When is a goodbye simply a goodbye? And when is it anything but—the smallest, the largest, the most literal, the most metaphoric, of deaths? In a 2019 article on the phenomenon of ghosting—that is,

ending a relationship without saying goodbye—a psychologist told *The New York Times* that ghosting has "a lot to do with someone's comfort level and how they deal with their emotions… you don't have a lot of accountability if you ghost someone." Our discomfort with confrontation is changing even how we *say* goodbye. In 2016, *Japan Today* reported that 80 percent of 20- to 30-year-olds now refrained from using the word "sayonara," preferring sign-offs that felt less final. "Saying 'sayonara' makes it seem like we won't meet again," explained one interviewee.

But is it really common sense to believe in the finality of an ending? Time makes fools of us all, eventually. And anyone who believes in the veracity of a farewell might be the biggest fool of all. Ex-friends and enemies will always pop up years later—at a party, on the train, in the anecdotes of someone new.

Even the most final goodbyes don't stick now—not with the internet around. "All My Exes Live in Texts" proclaimed a viral headline from a women's magazine some years ago, and it's true: Everyone from former lovers to departed pets is easily accessible, their photos and sometimes their words merely a keystroke away. The linear timeline has transformed into the formless online cloud. Perhaps this is why we continue to maintain digital connections with people from our past, however tenuous. We've always been uncomfortable with goodbyes, and now we can easily avoid them. No longer is dodging an adieu the coward's way out; today we can pretend the connection will remain—even though we know we're lying. "I am wedged between two tenses," writes Roland Barthes in *A Lover's Discourse*, from the perspective of the lover who is waiting, the lover who has been told goodbye. "You have gone (which I lament), you are here (since I'm addressing you)."

A goodbye is capricious: hasty you, foolhardy you, so certain that this is the end. Wait long enough, and all your goodbyes will come back to haunt you.

Even doctors struggle with final farewells. In his memoir *Do No Harm*, neurologist Henry Marsh admits to saying "good luck" rather than "goodbye" when leaving terminally ill patients.

KVADRAT/RAF SIMONS

A royal designing on the sleepy side of the Gulf.

Photography: Daniel Asater

JOHN CLIFFORD BURNS

Madiyah Al Sharqi

Al Sharqi is pictured wearing her own designs. Despite the burgeoning success of her fashion line, she maintains a low personal profile and chooses not to show her face in public images.

Madiyah Al Sharqi grew up as a member of the royal, ruling family of Fujairah—a small state in the United Arab Emirates, where strip malls and mid-rise office buildings sprawl under the foothills of a rugged mountain range. A princess who studied in Paris, Al Sharqi has since stayed put in her hometown—and brought a little pizazz to it with her flamboyant, eponymous fashion house. Her glamorous, 1970s-inspired designs, which include paisley lace trousers and red patent leather dresses, have since made it to pop-ups in Dubai and New York and into wardrobes all over Hollywood.

JCB: *Can you recall a pivotal moment in your upbringing that influenced your attitude to fashion?* **MAS:** My love for fashion started at a very early age and I mostly credit my mother for that. I remember her working closely with tailors to make bespoke pieces for her official engagements, and growing up around that made me realize early on that fashion and design was something I wanted to make a profession out of.

JCB: *Which item of clothing in your wardrobe holds the most sentimental value?* **MAS:** My grandmother's shawl from India—it's made from beige cashmere embroidered with paisley on the edges. It always makes me feel like she's still with me.

JCB: *What were your references when designing the AW19 collection?* **MAS:** AW19 is a broader story about the 1970s. Some of the most iconic women who've made a name for themselves in fashion and music came out of that decade, so it's been one of those periods I always find myself looking back to for inspiration. The collection has references to their adventurous attitude and bohemian style. They looked effortless but still very sophisticated, whether they were wearing a graphic printed blouse with a pair of flared leather pants during the day, or a sequined dress under a shearling coat for night.

JCB: *Are you a nostalgic person?* **MAS:** Yes, I am. I've always been fond of looking to the past as a source of inspiration for my collections, from referencing Marie Antoinette in my earliest seasons to Jacqueline Kennedy for Spring Summer 2019. But it's also very evident in a lot of my interests and hobbies—I appreciate reading classic novels, watching period plays and operas and traveling to places that hold a lot of rich history.

JCB: *What was the last thing you made with your hands?* **MAS:** A no-bake chocolate biscuit cake. It's one of my guilty pleasures and we've been making them since I was 12.

JCB: *What is the best piece of advice you've ever been given?* **MAS:** I've always stood by the advice to stay true to yourself in everything you say and do, and you'll find a way to fulfill something if it's important to you.

To Whom it May Concern

Five questions for an advice columnist.

When the answer to every question is just an internet search away, why do people still open their hearts to advice columnists? And what sort of person would dedicate themselves to answering strangers' pleas for guidance? For *Heather Havrilesky*, who had always loved to hand out advice, "it was this natural, bad, compulsive thing that I'd always been doing," she says. This inclination developed into a weekly advice column called Ask Polly—initially commissioned by *The Awl*, now a mainstay of *New York Magazine's* women's website, *The Cut*. Frank and sprinkled with humor, the column is a rallying cry to acceptance of our flawed and fragile selves. "Look closely at the things that embarrass you the most, and the things that get you in the most trouble," Havrilesky urges. "These are actually your finest qualities and your greatest charms."

PU: *Why do people often look to strangers for advice?* **HH:** It's difficult to ask good friends and family members for advice. There are very few people who are close enough to you, but have no stake in your decisions and only want you to serve yourself. When a friend says, "I think you should do X," it's hard to hear those instructions knowing what you know about that person. Not only do you assume that they know

things about you that are informing their advice, but you also know things about them that make you take their advice less seriously. Part of the joy of getting advice out of thin air is that you don't have clear access to the person who's writing it. Not knowing what my prejudices are, and how I screw up over and over again, it becomes much easier to take my advice.

PU: *How do you set about answering a letter?* **HH:** My writing tends to feel like a conversation with the person. I feel like I'm in the room with them, talking to them. By the same token, I'm not really in a discussion with them because they can't tell me more. And that's a convenience because it's a matter of looking at the letter itself.

When I started writing the column, I thought I'd have to consult the great philosophers and read a lot of psychology books. Actually, it's about trusting your gut and following simple ideas. It's not rocket science—I don't think I'm a genius or that I have the answers to everything. I just read a letter and find something in it and then think about the ramifications of that.

PU: *Is there a philosophical outlook that underpins your advice?* **HH:** Most people are trained in the art of beating themselves up. Excavating the layers of self-hatred and shame that we have crusted over us, and that run through our brains, is really difficult work. It

takes a long time and a lot of patience. But once you chip away at how self-defeating and self-destructive and pointlessly negative and hurtful these messages are that you feed yourself and that our culture feeds you, then you start to have a clear relationship with yourself. You start to have compassion for yourself, you start to have a feeling for life, and you start to understand how to savor the twisted pathways of your own messed-up mind to embrace exactly who you are. It's amazing how different the world looks once you dig through all your trash and throw it out.

PU: *What qualities are needed for your job?* **HH:** You have to be pushy, opinionated and a little bit crazy. You also have to be really interested in other people. I love getting mail from people that I don't know and listening to their issues and problems and confusions about their lives. Not everyone is interested in being dragged into other people's stories.

PU: *Does playing that role ever feel difficult?* **HH:** I'm a really emotional person, and I've become more emotional as I've gotten older, so it's like I'm playing with fire every day. But it's also the greatest thing in the world. I love doing what I do. I believe that everyone can be a lot happier than they are because I've lived it. It's important for me to bring all of my energy to spreading that hope.

Whereas many "sob sisters" pride themselves on writing snappy and humorous advice columns, Havrilesky's responses are long, personal and deeply empathetic.

Photograph: Ralph Morse/The LIFE Picture Collection/Getty Images

STARTERS

How to grumble with grace.

BEN SHATTUCK

On Complaining

A study conducted at Clemson University in South Carolina in 2014 showed that happier people tend to complain with a purpose, rather than grumbling for the sake of it.

The word "complain" comes from the medieval Latin *complangere*, "to bewail." And that's exactly how it sometimes feels. When the music is too loud in a restaurant, or a colleague keeps sneezing without covering his mouth, the urge is to howl out the injustice. And yet, so often we can't—social norms dictate that it would be too rude or aggressive to speak up. So we let the shrill guitar solo screech over the dinner date, or watch a cloud of virus-laden spittle swirl from a co-worker's lips. Why can't we bewail offenses freely?

Complaining is as old as time, and the modern, professional sort—the lawsuits Americans specialize in—is nearly medieval: The origin of nuisance laws can be traced to a case in the English countryside in 1610, when a man named William Aldred brought action against a pig farmer whose livestock produced "unpleasant odors" that reached the Aldreds' property. "One ought not have so delicate a nose that he cannot bear the smell of hogs," came the pig farmer's retort. This defense hints at the complainer's biggest fear: that the accused party will turn around and point out a weakness in the character of their accuser. One ought not have so delicate a nose for pigs, or such anxiety for a little sneeze. When contemplating complaining, one goes through a small ethical crisis, trying to decide what type of person they are,

if they are relaxed enough to let something slide or too highly strung. One of the most revealing linguistic elements of a complaint is the fact that we "lodge" it—as in, *you must lodge a complaint against the airline that lost your bags for three weeks, and then delivered them to the hotel where you were no longer staying.* To lodge a complaint is to make it foundational and immovable, as if you're excavating the fine topsoil of social etiquette to pour a heavy load of dissatisfaction into the ground of whichever waiter or airline customer service representative is on the other side. But that's exactly the way it should be thought of. Instead of the softer *venting* we all do ("I don't like that restaurant"), you should be specific: "Next time we go that restaurant I'm going to ask them to turn down the music."

If you want to successfully complain, psychologist and author Guy Winch writes in his book *The Squeaky Wheel*, first be sure it's a valid complaint, then have a deliberate purpose of outcome and finally be kind to the person you're complaining to. If that person becomes defensive, if they can't separate a polite request from a personal attack, then go to another restaurant or bring it to their boss. It's not your job to manage someone's feelings, and certainly not your duty to withstand injustice. In the end, "One ought not have so delicate a nose" is no defense.

Photography: Rala Choi for Gentle Monster

MINI METAPHORS

by Pip Usher

There's great pleasure derived from a dollhouse in good order; the owner is granted power over a tiny domestic realm. But what happens if frightening truths from the outside world start to penetrate? It's an idea explored to chilling effect in horror hits like *Hereditary* and *The Haunting of Hill House*, where the dollhouse becomes the stage on which the horrors suffered by its owner are played out in miniature. Psychological torture, abuse, even murder: These macabre depictions of human violence subvert a dollhouse's innocence into something terrible. As much as we try to exert control, we too are helpless— just like the dolls trapped inside. (Top: Miniature Zig Zag Stool by Vitra Design Museum at Paustian. Center: Landmarks Bookends by Klemens Schillinger. Bottom: Green Ride-on Vehicle at Gollnest & Kiesel.)

CHARLES SHAFAIEH

Small Matters

The big appeal of tiny things.

In his phenomenological study of architecture, *The Poetics of Space*, philosopher Gaston Bachelard describes a key difference between how the minuscule and the gigantic engage our minds. "A bit of moss may well be a pine, but a pine will never be a bit of moss," he writes. "The imagination does not function with the same conviction in both directions." By serving to conjure possible worlds, tiny items have become objects of fascination and even obsession throughout history, from portraits gifted as signs of affection in Tudor and Stuart England to dollhouses and Legos used by children as toys or educational tools.

The otherworldliness of miniatures manifests itself in myriad ways. Stuffed animals and action figures turn into children's friends as narratives are created around them. By contrast, adult toys, like historic-battlefield playsets or more modern games like *The Sims*, might be attractive for the power they let people wield over fantasylands. The godlike sense of control they engender can deflect life's uncontrollable chaos.

Yet miniatures that demand a relinquishment of power, such as those connected to spiritual realms, are also enticing. Consider the carvings made by the Zuni people of present-day New Mexico. Sometimes as small as a fingernail, these figures, called fetishes, are crafted from turquoise and other stones. Zuni mythology holds that the correspondent spirit animal resides within them and in turn can imbue their holder with their traits. The bear, for example, acts as a strong protector, while the coyote is a trickster.

It is not just physical miniatures—whether fetishes or Fabergé eggs—that spark the imagination. Most mimetic art involves miniaturization. Writers condense objects into a few words, draftsmen rarely work to scale and television squeezes people into screens.

It is no surprise, then, that early cinema is replete with shrinking effects, including a 1903 adaptation of Lewis Caroll's *Alice's Adventures in Wonderland*. While just 12 minutes long, the film centers on the scene in which a fan makes Alice small, thus allowing her—and her audience—to begin a journey through a small door that, like much art, opens to undiscovered worlds.

Photograph: Dima Hohlov for Max V. Koenig

Same Same, But Different

The mystery of conflicting memories.

You might have heard the 1,000-year-old story of two blind men wanting to know what an elephant looks like: The one who touches the trunk imagines and describes a very different animal than the one who leans on the stomach, pets the ear, hugs a leg. They argue over who is right, though we know they are both simultaneously right and wrong.

The Rashomon effect—the phenomenon of recounting the same event differently—comes from the title of the 1950 Japanese film by Akira Kurosawa, in which four witnesses remember the circumstances around the death of a samurai in four different ways. The samurai's wife claimed she was sexually assaulted by a bandit, passed out and then awoke to find her husband dead. The bandit claimed he *seduced* the wife and then killed the samurai in a duel—and so on. The dramatic tension tightens around the fault of memory: Should the viewer side with one story, or are all four part of a single truth? The term drifted into academia in the 1960s after researchers saw that memory wilts under the power of suggestion, assumption or personal history. Different people experience the world in different ways, and so they cannot share in the same objective memories.

Remembering things differently is seed for fiction, poison for courts, scaffolding for gossip. The same event can be endlessly interpreted in multiple ways because reality—so say neurologists—isn't consistent.

Cousins of the Rashomon effect are staples in fiction: the unreliable narrator; chapter-by-chapter rotating point of views; limited perspectives. There is, for instance, the scene in Ian McEwan's *Atonement* when young Briony sees a man bully her older sister to undress and dip into a fountain. Later, we see this same event from the sister's perspective, showing that she is, in fact, the one in control. The gap in perspective between Briony and her sister will make all the difference in the characters' lives. Many stories depend on characters getting it wrong. The most famous might be Humbert Humbert in Vladimir Nabokov's *Lolita*: What he sees as a love trip through the American landscape, Lolita might remember as kidnapping and sexual slavery.

But literature suggests that there is an objective reality. You can find the truth of an event simply by looking at how the author represents and leaves the characters. Nabokov shows his narrator's perspective as a twisted one, full of violence and self-deception; Humbert Humbert will only trick a naive and inattentive reader. Ian McEwan lets Briony's incorrect recollection plow a path toward sadness, guilt and solitude for all the characters. It's satisfying to think that there exists a clean memory that can be shared and understood by the characters to allow them—and the reader—a revelation. In real life, however, we must settle for only having the blind certainty of our own conviction.

Rashomon has been described as an allegory for Japan's defeat in World War II; the film is about differing memories of a deadly fight.

Photography: Zoltan Tombor

The Iranian-American filmmaker bringing her "weird and sexy" stories—and her parents—to set.

MEGAN NOLAN

Desiree Akhavan

Desiree Akhavan is not very good at taking time off. "Right now I'm upstate with my ex-girlfriend, dogsitting. Yesterday, we went on a hike and the whole time I wanted to talk about writing my book and how to shape a chapter, and she was like, 'Maybe you should write about how you can't enjoy a vacation,'" says Akhavan, speaking from her temporary hideout in New York's Catskill Mountains.

The Iranian-American filmmaker is as busy as ever, but in a way she's never been before: on her own. She's currently writing her first book, a collection of essays, after making her name as a groundbreaking writer, director and producer of films and television. *Appropriate Behavior* was her first feature film, made in 2014 with production partner Cecilia Frugiuele, about a headstrong Iranian-American bisexual woman grappling with heartbreak. *The Miseducation of Cameron Post* followed in 2018—an empathetic and nuanced story about gay conversion therapy in the US. In the same year, her smart, hilarious television show *The Bisexual* aired on Channel 4 in the UK, inspired by Akhavan's own discomfort with the label. Whatever Akhavan lends her talents to, she finds a grateful audience for her startling, frank voice on queerness and female desire.

MN: *You're currently working on a collection of essays. How does it feel to be working on something on your own, rather than as part of a larger film or TV production?* **DA:** It's the worst. I really don't want to write prose ever again. I think there's something really special about the collaborative nature of writing and making films. It's a different muscle and one I prefer. I think some people perfect things by themselves; they're good at analyzing it from all angles. I find that I have to analyze it from every angle with a handful of people I trust, and without their brains, I don't really know what I have.

MN: *Do you engage in that sort of group analysis when screening early cuts of films?* **DA:** Yeah. When we made *The Miseducation of Cameron Post* we had a ridiculously large number of public screenings. It really needed a lot of cuts and edits. A tangible example of how that worked was the scene where Cameron finds Mark's blood. Before, that scene was very cut and dried and it never really hit you in the gut. It was never a tough moment, and we had this feeling of, "How do we make this matter?" "How do you raise the stakes when you only have this footage to pull from?" But then our editor Sarah intercut the scene of Mark having the breakdown with Cameron finding the blood. And once she intercut them, it had real emotional effect. I learned a lot about what it is to make a movie, and to be emotionally manipulative.

MN: *When you were working on your first film,* Appropriate Behavior, *did you find it difficult to assume a leadership role on set, especially as a woman?* **DA:** No, not at all.

MN: *And why is that?* **DA:** 'Cause I'm a fucking boss! In the book, I'm writing about what it is to direct. And I think it's about opening yourself up and being super in touch with every single person on your set and what they need. And everyone needs something a little bit different. That's what it is to be a leader. I really get off on it, and I don't think that's for everybody.

MN: *How does it feel being written up as cool now? You've spoken before about having been a lonely, awkward child.* **DA:** It feels absurd. But I also feel very young right now. I'm 34 and I just moved back to New York a month ago. A friend of mine likes to go to clubs until the sun comes out. I've been going out with him, and it really shocks me that I've never felt as young and carefree as I do right now. There's a freedom in getting older. It's like, I don't think anyone's judging me or watching me now or if they are, I really don't give a shit. Whereas when you're younger, I think you have this narrative of shame and this voice in your head that's constantly going, "Are you sure you're doing that?" "You sure you're not fucking that up?"

MN: *Can you identify a time in your life when you grew that confidence, where you transitioned from that sad child to being assured?* **DA:** I mean, it's so sad to have to point to this as the catalyst, but everything about my life has been dictated by the work I do—in terms of my joy, or my sadness. When the work is going well, I feel alive and right. And when it's not going well, I don't know how to function.

MN: *Were your parents supportive of your career choices?* **DA:** They were really supportive. I was lucky. I did my first play at 12 and it was a big deal, because before it I felt very mediocre in all aspects of life. I tried very hard but did very

"It would be hard to deny your sad kid the one thing they're great at."

badly at school, and was such a sad, sad kid. It wasn't until I was on stage that my parents really saw me come alive. I think it would be hard to deny your sad kid the one thing they're great at.

MN: *Are you permanently back in New York now?* **DA:** Honestly, I don't think I'll be anywhere permanently. You go where the work takes you. And unless I had a kid, I think I would always be like that. I'm in New York right now, I have a place, but I'm also about to go to work with Cecilia [Frugiuele, her creative partner] in Italy for a month and then go to shoot something in New Mexico for another month.

MN: *What are you working on with Cecilia?* **DA:** She's coming out here tomorrow to interview some of my family members with me. It's a film project inspired by my parents' life during the Islamic Revolution. My mom got married at 19 and fled [Iran] a year later with a newborn, so we're thinking about how to tell that story. It's very much about the sacrifices women make for family. That's certainly something I'm thinking about—I'm 34, I really want children, but I don't have a partner.

I think it's going to be really good and also really weird and sexy. I'm excited to see those things alongside any Iranian narrative, but it's also intimidating as fuck, because I never lived in Iran. It's a culture and a language that's been handed down to me, so it's sort of like playing a game of telephone. I'm so used to making things that are personal, and this is so personal, but it's also stepping into something larger than myself, because it's connected to war.

MN: *Is your mom happy to speak with you about leaving Iran?* **DA:** I think that parents, especially Iranian parents, would throw themselves in front of a bus for you. So if you're like, "This is what I need for my work," then they will do that for you. My mom and dad used to drive the trucks to my set. My mom would cook and my dad would be a grip. And now, even though they're very private people and don't necessarily love having their business broadcast, they understand. This work connects me to my family and, as much as it's probably annoying for them to to be exposed in certain ways, I think they all respect that. Or maybe I'm just an asshole egomaniac. But I love that I get to ask these questions I've been wondering about my entire life for the sake of work.

Akhavan's work approaches the question of what it means to "fit in" from multiple angles. *The Bisexual* is a comedy that considers why so many bi women find the label to be awkward or even embarrassing.

2
Features

Waris

Kyla Marshell chronicles the many marvelous lives of *Waris Ahluwalia.*

Jewelry designer. Wes Anderson regular. Environmental crusader.

Photography by Zoltan Tombor & Styling by Jermaine Daley

FEATURES

Grooming: Alana Wright

As he tells it, Waris Ahluwalia was just walking down the street when fortune found him. He was in Los Angeles, wearing diamond rings of his own design, and had stepped into the high-end store Maxfield when his work caught the eye of their buyer. He was then in his late twenties. The meeting that would launch his career as a jewelry designer, and his company, House of Waris, was not the culmination of years of training in design or metalworking. This part of his story—there are many parts—smacks of that classic trope: Big shot discovers new talent and the rest is history.

How Ahluwalia went from making jewelry, to acting in films, to where he is now—working with conservationist organizations to protect elephant populations in Asia—is a winding path with an invisible compass. "To some degree, I was lucky," he says. "But I chose to go down that path. Nothing was handed to me."

Ahluwalia gets the question "What do you do?" fairly often. He's been called a Renaissance man, a polymath, a multi-hyphenate actor/activist/designer/dandy/man-about-town; but labels, he believes, are more about the labeler, than the labeled. "We take them on and then that becomes our construct. So I try not to have a construct."

He is tall, lanky, handsome, and often dressed in bespoke suits; or, today, in the sunny backyard of the café and clothing store Hesperios in New York City, in a sweatshirt and jeans that somehow still stand out. You may recognize him from one of his many roles as an actor—in Wes Anderson's *The Life Aquatic with Steve Zissou* and *The Grand Budapest Hotel*; Spike Lee's *Inside Man*; and most recently, Natasha Lyonne's Netflix series *Russian Doll*. Or perhaps you saw him on the news: In 2013, an ad he appeared in for the Gap prompted a conversation about racial and religious prejudice after it was defaced with racist comments; and, in 2016, media outlets covered his detention at Mexico City International Airport after he refused to remove his turban, a religious article for Sikh men. In New York, and elsewhere, he is a fixture at parties and fashion shows. His is the kind of amorphous public persona that might irk someone determined to be known only for the seriousness of their work. Such a perception doesn't seem to bother him. "The outside world gets confused unless you have a role to play," he says.

Ahluwalia was born in Amritsar, Punjab, India, in 1974, and moved with his parents to the south Brooklyn neighborhood of Bay Ridge when he was five. He attended the prestigious Brooklyn Tech High School, but when he thought about what he wanted to do afterward, he drew a blank. "I think that's probably what led to me wanting to do everything [in my career]," he says. "I think it's as a result of having no clue, early on."

He attended Marist College, a small liberal arts school in upstate New York, pursuing a degree that matched his indecision—general studies. "My process was elimination, trying things and going, 'Oh, that's not for me.' Biology class in ninth grade, and walking out of the class and thinking, 'There's no way I'm going to be a doctor.'"

But there was one thing that had already piqued his interest—he just couldn't major in it. Like many New York City teenagers with easy access to transportation, Ahluwalia found himself in famed clubs such as the Limelight and Save the Robots, where he and his similarly underage friends danced until the wee hours. It was New York in the early '90s, before the M&M store became a central landmark of Times Square, and the nightlife—club kids and drag queens, strobe lights and smoke machines, extravagant costumes handmade for the occasion—is what he remembers as the first thing he was drawn to, a hint of how he might spend his life.

Though partying is certainly a common activity, for most, it's not a job. But it makes perfect sense as the central passion of Ahluwalia's life—the free-form creativity that would later solidify into a recognizable shape. After college, he once again found himself up late, out and about, in a community of creative souls, all trying to find their way in life and in the arts. It was those connections that helped him whittle down the infinity of possibilities he'd laid out for himself.

"If you can imagine, it's 3 a.m. in a dark room in a club and you're sitting with friends and all of a sudden [whatever you're talking about] becomes a movie idea or a book idea," he recalls. "There was less pressure, because you were just trying things, and it wasn't yet available for the world to see and share."

Ahluwalia needed inspiration, in part, because the first thing he'd tried had become dispiriting and untenable. He'd started a nonprofit geared toward educating young South Asians on safe sex and AIDS, with music and entertainment as the vehicle. Activism, with a spoonful of sugar. But as any nonprofit administrator knows, running such a fledgling enterprise is a challenge on all fronts. "It was such an uphill battle," he recalls. "I was like, 'There has to be a better way to make change. This is just too slow.'"

Waris wears a sweater by Lacoste.

"The outside world gets confused unless you have a role to play."

Below: Waris wears a sweater by
Ermenegildo Zegna and trousers by
Todd Snyder. Right: He wears a suit
by The Row, a T-shirt by A.P.C. and
socks by Falke.

After the many ideas he'd thrown at the wall, the thing that stuck was jewelry—dazzling rings and earrings and pendants, like those brilliant costumes he'd once seen on the dance floor. He drew a design; a friend of a friend took it to a manufacturer. Those free-flowing, twilight conversations had yielded something he could hold.

Entering the design world, he wanted to marry the yin and yang of his life: partying and purpose, celebration and humanity. Jewelry, he hoped, would allow him to do that. He saw it as a means of pursuing collaborations with friends—of taking his relationships beyond the dinner table. House of Waris became that platform. The company later expanded into textiles, and has hosted numerous fundraisers and pop-up projects. Ahluwalia's jewelry has sold in stores such as Barney's, Bergdorf Goodman, Colette, and Dover Street Market; he created a line for Forevermark. But for the last five years, Ahluwalia has been on what he calls a "sabbatical" from making jewelry.

Unlike most designers, he visited the mines from which jewels for his pieces were sourced. At one point, he was spending six months of the year in India, working daily with craftspeople, living with them, getting to know their families. There were no factories; the prices, which started at $2,000, were set by the craftspeople, quantified by their skill and labor, as well as the rarity of the stones used. He never sold to a store before visiting it. He is very confident and very clear: His company did not exploit its workers. But was it exploiting the earth?

"Our very existence is exploitation of the planet," he explains. "Do you use a fork when you eat? It comes from mining. Regardless of the fact that I was lucky enough to be selling in the best stores in the world, I just wasn't comfortable living with that disconnect."

It wasn't enough that he'd been to the mines, that the craftspeople had been properly compensated, that he was fastidious about following the chain of custody from the pit of the earth to the front of the store. There's something about selling a $60,000 pair of earrings that can make even the most conscientious designer question their values. And if he was telling the truth, which he was committed to doing, no matter what, he actually couldn't be sure where every element had originated. All he knew was that these resources belonged to nature, and humans—his least favorite animal—had grown wild in their entitlement to them.

He also realized that he had inadvertently put himself into rarified air. "The worst was when people would come up to me and say, 'One

"Humans tend to lean towards fear; it's the easiest thing that they can attach to."

day I hope to afford your jewelry,'" he recalls. "And I was like, 'No, if you can't afford it, don't worry about it. There are better things to aspire to.' But I was part of that same cycle now. I was part of that cycle of creating want in a very materialistic world."

It was time to take a break.

Though Ahluwalia misses drawing and spending time with craftspeople, stepping back from design has freed him up to focus more on conservation. It's something he's passionate about, speaking in detail about what he calls "the human, planetary crisis." Tangibly, that crisis is the ongoing destruction of our planet—not just climate change, but deforestation, overdevelopment and widespread killing of plant and animal species. Intellectually, it's our collective unawareness of what the problem is: us.

For more than a decade, Ahluwalia has worked with the London-based nonprofit Elephant Family, whose mission, in part, is to facilitate coexistence between humans and elephants across Asia. "Human beings are terrible, terrible creatures," he says with a laugh. When it comes to, say, elephant poaching, he points out that the messaging is all wrong. "It's easier, as individuals, to think the problem is poaching, because there are bad guys and there are victims. But the overall problem is the fact that creatures in the wild are running out of wild spaces. [Humans'] very existence threatens the existence of all species because we require so many natural resources."

He discovered Elephant Family while he was working with Wes Anderson on *The Darjeeling Limited*. Anderson asked him to make a pin that his character, a train steward, would wear on his uniform. Ahluwalia made an elephant, then searched for a charity to donate the proceeds to after he sold the pins commercially. And so began another collaboration, another celebration of life. The organization employs a team of conservationists who devise ways to protect the vulnerable elephant population from the conflicts that human presence has created. Ahluwalia's official title is that of patron, a role that has encompassed fund- and consciousness-raising in the United States. In their most recent annual report, Elephant Family thanked him for his "guidance and friendship, together with his acute sense of aesthetics [that] have powered Elephant Family in so many inspiring ways."

The awareness he wants to encourage goes beyond the particular issues facing wildlife. "Over time, we've been removed from ourselves,

from each other, to create 'the other,'" he says. "[First] the other is another human being, then the other becomes wildlife, becomes nature. We look at it as separate things when it needs to just be one." This conviction is why, in the wake of the Gap ad defacement and his detainment in Mexico City, he felt a responsibility to speak to the wider issue of racial prejudice, drawing parallels between his own experience and the message behind Black Lives Matter.

"Humans tend to lean towards fear; it's the easiest thing that they can attach to," he said on the UK's Channel 4 news program, shortly after the airport incident in Mexico. "The opposite is love, which takes nurturing and care, so it's a lot more work."

Love over fear; integrity over profit; unity over division: Ahluwalia knows these are challenging mandates. But beyond the injustice itself, he wants to find a more appealing way to present the issues. He is, after all, a designer. He is not being flip when he says, "We're all dying. It's okay. But how do we get past that? How do we celebrate?"

Ahluwalia's next celebration is a line of organic teas and beverages, sourced from around the world. As when he went to the diamond mines or designed jewelry for an acting role that could also be a gift to charity, this project is about collaboration and maintaining a sense of innate wholeness. It's also a way to make a product that is more affordable and accessible than his jewelry. He has been visiting tea estates around the world, seeing where the leaves are grown, cut and dried, and helping the estates' proprietors convert their land into elephant-friendly territories.

"I'm forever trying to find how to give back with the action that you're doing so it's not an afterthought. The only way to make change is that what we're doing now has to be part of the solution—it has to be built into the doing."

Celebration and humanity. On a recent visit to his mother's home in Brooklyn, he was reminded just how much those twin flames have meant to him. Rooting around, he found a flyer for a rave he and a friend had thrown in Manchester, while studying abroad in the UK. He'd forgotten all about the party, called Love Life. At the bottom of the flyer, it said, "All proceeds go to anti-racist causes." It was a missive from his past saying, *This is who you've always been.*

"We're all dying," he says again. "But if we can do it while we're dancing? I don't see the harm in that."

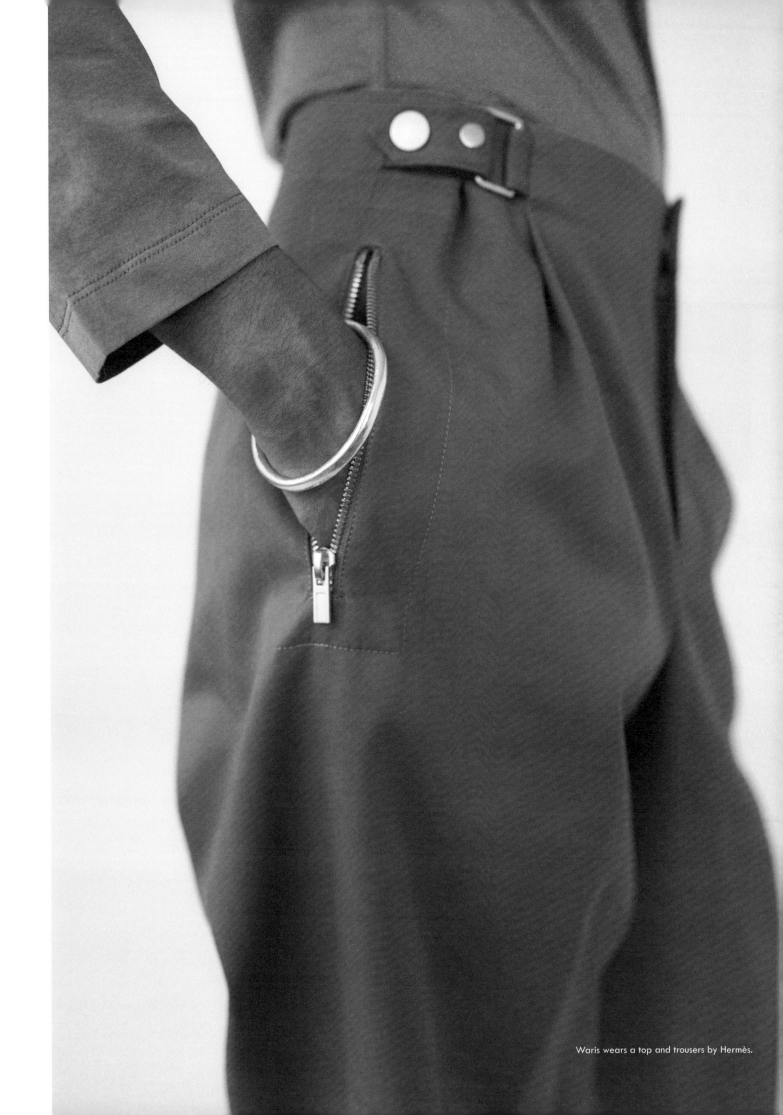

Waris wears a top and trousers by Hermès.

Day in the Life:
Michaël Borremans

At a château-turned-studio in rural Belgium, *Annick Weber* meets the enigmatic artist whose twisted imagination is revitalizing figurative painting. Photography by *Marsý Hild Þórsdóttir*

"Can you believe this used to be a car park?" Michaël Borremans asks, looking out onto the vast expanse of greenery unfolding before him. It's hard to picture the daisy-dotted back garden of the painter's countryside studio covered in a blanket of concrete. And yet, such was the case nine years ago, when Borremans bought the 19th-century property—formerly a baron's hunting château—as a rural alternative to his primary studio in Ghent. Today, the site is a tableau of serenity. Ancient trees tower in the distance, and horses graze around them. "A lot of the trees are in their last phase, so I planted some new ones," Borremans says, pointing to a row of young saplings across the lawn. "You have to make sure that future generations have their trees too."

One of the most acclaimed figurative painters in Europe, Borremans knows a thing or two about creating a legacy. Born in Belgium in 1963, he turned to painting in the mid-1990s after training in graphic arts and a stint working as a photographer and art school teacher. "I already had a certain control over form and light, I just had to teach myself how to work with colors and the materiality of paint," he says of his transition. "I started off with things that I could master; a hand or face would have been too hard." It took five years for Borremans to develop his con-

fidence, and find a figurative language that was truly his own. At the time, the city's Municipal Museum of Contemporary Art had just opened a new offsite space in Ghent, where he landed a solo show in 2000. The founder of the museum acquired a work and interest from galleries and museums around the world followed soon after. Now, he says, "My paintings get snatched away as soon as I finish one."

Borremans paints people, but not portraits. He depicts anonymous sitters who look somehow absent, their eyes never meeting those of the viewer. Hooded figures stand frozen as if consumed by some mysterious ritualistic force. Children clasp objects—a missile, a dead hare, a bunch of carrots—that could be mistaken for toys, were it not for the gruesome or absurd connotations they carry. Sometimes, his sitters' features are blown into grotesque proportions. "My work is two things at the same time: It's holding a mirror onto the complex, often dark facets of human nature while borrowing a very familiar vocabulary of classic portraiture," Borremans explains. "It's contradictory and it's alienating the beholder, and that's the fun of it."

Borremans likes to keep his distance in life, as well as art. He bought this second studio-home in the countryside because he

Borremans was once described by curator Jeffrey Grove as a "pop artist": His unsettling depictions of torture and violence hold up a dark mirror to the media we consume on a daily basis.

longed for a place where he could paint in peace. "I'm a loner," he notes. As well as granting solitude, the sheer size of the property—one floor with a dozen rooms, a barn, an attic "for large-scale works" and a large park-garden "to watch the wildlife"—gives him enough space that he can leave his paintings alone. "The whole house is a studio, which means that I can lock up a work in one room and move on to something else until I'm ready to go back," Borremans says. Each room has an atmosphere of its own. One resembles a traditional painting studio with easels and map cabinets filled with paper drawings, while others blur the boundaries between working and living—semi-finished canvases rest on windowsills, and painting tools are scattered around dining tables. The interior teems with oddities—a taxidermic badger here, a vintage toy farm there.

Borremans' process is meticulous and unusual. To start each new piece, he has models come to his studio and pose for him, awkwardly holding a prop. He compares these bizarre, staged situations to theater. Rather than painting from these live models, however, Borremans photographs the scenes and uses the shots as sketches for his work. "These photo shoots are a crucial step in my process," he says. "I try a lot of things in them; they allow me to check whether a composition is working in terms of space and light."

When Borremans works in his countryside studio, he likes going for walks around the grounds to clear his mind, though sometimes he's so absorbed that he forgets to take breaks. Other times, the most productive sessions can happen in 15 minutes. His ideal is to be like "a dandy, who starts working without realizing it," he says, biting into a piece of flan tart. It's late afternoon, and this is the first time he's eaten today. "When I'm into a painting, it becomes my life, and my studio—my microcosmos," he continues. "I get obsessed with things happening beyond my control. Having a plan is dangerous,

it produces these clean, uptight results. But being open to taking risks when working with paint, that's what brings energy into it all." Borremans' voice is calm. He often pauses before speaking, taking the time to ponder. "I revere old artists who painted very quickly, like Goya and Caravaggio," he says. "In their work, the paint itself tells a story."

Borremans' admiration of the Old Masters shines through in his technique, which combines the multilayered approach of his Flemish forefathers with the desaturated color palette of the Spanish Baroque and the firm brushstrokes of early Impressionism. Art history books are piled on coffee tables, desks, floors and shelves. But while his style references the classical canon, Borremans' subject matter—power, race, gender and religion—situates his paintings firmly within the 21st century. "Many painters copy ancient techniques and the result looks ancient too," he says. "There's a lot of boring work in the world. It may sound arrogant, but I think mine is not." Art is a way of "dealing with existence," he says. "People say my art is cruel, but it's just how humans are. We can all be cannibals under certain circumstances. We all have good and bad inside us." But it's no wonder that viewers might ask the question: His 2017 series *Fire from the Sun* shows naked toddlers, sometimes missing a limb, sometimes covered in a blood-like substance.

Back outside in the garden, Borremans has taken a seat under the sprawling canopy of an oak tree. One of its giant branches is resting on a metal structure he built for support. "We try and help him wherever we can," he says, looking up at the fragile branch. But the idyll is short-lived. Seconds later he admits to the silliness of his intervention into nature: "We don't even know if he wants to live," he says. "Who knows, maybe he's suffering." If Borremans were to make a painting of the scene, the metal brace would surely be the prop that his subject is absurdly clinging on to.

Both Borremans' countryside retreat and his house in Ghent are filled with odd objects that interest him, some of which are used as props in his paintings.

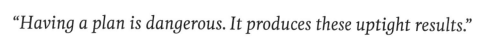

"Having a plan is dangerous. It produces these uptight results."

"People say my art is cruel, but it's just how humans are."

Borremans' desaturated color palette is in part the result of his artistic roots in the black and white world of pencil drawing.

THE GREAT INFLUENCE SCAM

TEXT:
DEBIKA RAY

Hey lovelies! Are you interested in an incredible business opportunity that gives you the ability to work from home? For decades now, network marketing companies have been dangling the promise of a rocketing income, flexible schedule and aspirational lifestyle in front of people desperate for a lucky break. But what happens when the dream of direct sales starts to look more like a nightmare? Debika Ray investigates.

"I was in a religious cult in my youth—so I quickly recognized the feeling," says Charlotte over a confidential internet call from Australia. She does not want to divulge her full name because, she says, the subjects of this discussion are highly litigious. Charlotte is part of the Anti-MLM Coalition—a group of activists striving to educate people about multi-level marketing. Also known as network marketing, multi-level marketing is a business model—popularized by the likes of Avon and Tupperware in the middle of the last century—under which a brand's products are sold through a network of unsalaried representatives. The representatives buy discounted stock to resell and are remunerated through a system of commissions on their transactions and those of anyone they enlist as fellow distributors. It's a business model that has thrived for decades but one that is laden with insights into the gendered nature of consumerism and the power of social media to muddy the waters between social and transactional relationships.

Charlotte signed up in 2016 to sell a range of liquid lipsticks after a friend who was already doing so pointed out that she would get a discount on the products if she enrolled as a distributor. She lasted about five months before withdrawing, put off primarily by the interactions she witnessed on the secret Facebook groups she was added to by her "upline"—the person who recruited her. "It's hard to put into words," Charlotte says. "It's very much like high

school girl, *Mean Girls* sort of stuff. There's a lot of adulation of the CEO, the woman who started the MLM, and that is quite typical because the founder is seen with almost religious fervor so there was nothing she could say that was wrong."

The term "pyramid scheme" is often used to describe these kinds of groups, but MLM chains are not technically pyramid schemes. For one thing, they are legal in most jurisdictions—although many argue that they should at least be better regulated. For another, most involve selling tangible products and services, rather than investment opportunities.

Far from ringing alarm bells, for many people the names Avon (which has been operating since 1886) and Tupperware (since 1948) evoke cozy images of groups of women gathered around the kitchen table sharing conversation and advice over tea and cake, making harmless, small-scale purchases from each other and sometimes going on to become "Avon ladies" or host Tupperware parties themselves. A myriad of other brands, selling everything from sex toys to dog food, earn billions operating in a similar way. Big names include American companies Amway (health, beauty and homeware products), Herbalife (dietary supplements), LuLaRoe (clothing) and Mary Kay (cosmetics); German firm Vorwerk (household appliances, kitchen and beauty products) and Hong Kong-based Infinitus (Chinese herbal health products). According to the Direct Sell-

ing Association, which represents the industry, in 2017 there were 18.6 million direct-selling representatives in the US—where most of these businesses are based—up from 15 million in 2007. MLMs account for about $34.9 billion in sales. Many now operate in other developed countries, as well as in countries with growing consumer markets such as India and Mexico. The trouble is, according to research, the practice is less about selling products than about roping other people into doing it, too.

Multi-level marketing has taken on a new life in the social media era, with platforms such as Facebook, YouTube and Instagram giving distributors new channels through which to market their stock and win over recruits. Younique, for example—founded in 2012—boasts of being "the first direct sales company to market and sell almost exclusively through the use of social media," through its "virtual parties." "My most successful parties are when the hostess invites between 200 and 300 people," says one blog by a network marketer, advising others to post regularly on their own personal page, as well as within groups they specifically set up for MLM sales. It's perhaps no surprise that social media, much of which is built around personal image and branding and careful self-presentation, lends itself so well to MLM —especially when brands are increasingly keen to tap into the power of "influencers."

Many opposed to MLM complain of their feeds being inundated by friends selling essential oils or dietary supplements, as well as photos depicting the glamorous lifestyle that supposedly comes with climbing the ladder within one of these organizations—photos of designer items, sports cars and luxury holidays are signifiers of their success. Partly because of this, the practice of MLM has attracted vociferous opposition—the "antiMLM" group on Reddit has over 470,000 members, while *The Dream* podcast recently caused a stir with its investigation into the world of MLM—including its impact on women. The objections go beyond mere annoyance—many point to the financial and psychological damage these schemes can do.

Their strongest argument comes from independent researcher Jon M. Taylor's 2011 report for the Federal Trade Commission, the US consumer protection agency: Taylor concluded that 99% of MLM promoters take a loss after expenses. This is partly because distributors often buy up their own stock to meet the targets needed to qualify for commissions. "Often you need to sell a minimum amount—for example, £500 worth of products," says Hannah Martin, who runs the Talented Ladies Club, a British website and service which helps new mothers back into work, and has been investigating MLMs for the past few years. "If you don't meet that target, you become 'inactive' and have to buy a starter kit—the initial minimum investment in stock—again."

Taylor points out that the business model is largely insular and dependent on purchases by distributors themselves, rather than by people outside the line of business—essentially shifting money from newer entrants to a few at the top. This means that distributors are heavily incentivized and trained to recruit, which chimes with the findings of Jane Marie, host of *The Dream* podcast. "The product you're selling doesn't really matter," she says. "The goal of all these companies is to find sitting ducks who will say, 'Yes, sign me up,' then who cares

if there's a market for whatever you're selling?" MLM businesses refute these claims. One blog—believed by many to be from an affiliate of the Direct Selling Association—asks why "92 million people around the world" would continue to take part in a business if losses are almost guaranteed. And it's certainly not the case that people have universally bad experiences. One woman who has been selling Younique products for almost four years tells me that MLM is attractive because it's cheap to start up and, if the product is good, your only limit is yourself. "The people who don't like them are usually those who thought they would be millionaires overnight and who just didn't do the work that was necessary."

But Robert Fitzpatrick, president of consumer campaign Pyramid Scheme Alert, says the very foundation is false: "The 'opportunity' is not 'unlimited,'" he writes in one paper. "It is finite and diminishing. The thousands at the bottom of the pyramid cannot possibly enroll as many recruits as those few at the top already have." Taylor echoes this: "MLM as a business model is the epitome of an 'unfair or deceptive acts or practice.' MLM makes even gambling look like a safe bet in comparison."

And the impact is not just financial, says Charlotte. Getting involved can be psychologically and socially damaging, often affecting personal relationships. "The typical pattern seems to be one partner in a couple joins an MLM, gets very involved and heavily invested, develops new social circles, their personality changes and they spend increasing amounts on MLM products and training, dropping 'non-supportive' friends and family and increasing conflict when the other partner has concerns. We've also heard of university students abandoning their studies to work in MLMs full time." It's easy to see why it would be a nuisance to have your friends unexpectedly treat you like a customer or potential recruit, and why do-

ing so might damage your relationships. But the pressure to succeed and the incentive not to quit, Charlotte says, is reinforced by the way distributors present themselves on social media. "Distributors are encouraged to 'fake it 'til you make it,'" she says. "There's a culture of overstating your earnings and you're encouraged to sell a lifestyle, which most of them are not actually living." The intention is to inspire newer entrants to stick with it, with promises of rewards—fancy cars and vacations—if you rise up the ranks to the likes of "black" or "platinum" status. The Talented Ladies Club has pulled together examples of distributors saying things online like, "Make your Facebook think your business is booming—even if you've only had one order."

So if MLM can be so damaging, why does it continue to attract people? That's difficult to answer because of the lack of academic research into MLMs and transparency by the companies around their practices. But it's also at least partly because of who such businesses target (or rather, who their independent representatives target, because instructions rarely seem to be linked to the companies themselves). Marie is cautious about attributing it to a personality type, but she says she noticed that responses during her research for *The Dream* tended to fall into two camps. "People were either immediately suspicious or they were fully on board. Those who are interested truly believe that they will be that one percent who succeed." More specifically, she says, reps strive to recruit people in particular life circumstances. "They look in communities where they feel they'll have a good chance of converting believers with the promises of wealth and freedom," she says. "It's definitely marketed to people who have few other options for work and for making a living, and for whom their lives are already pretty restricted." Charlotte has a similar assessment: "They are

"It's perhaps no surprise that social media, much of which is built around personal image and branding and careful self-presentation, lends itself so well to multi-level marketing."

presenting an opportunity to people who are having a rough time or don't have enough money—young moms at home, people with disabilities or chronic illness, retirees, immigrants who haven't been able to work because of visas, military wives, freelancers, students."

Martin adds that, in her experience, reps are encouraged to pounce on people if they catch sight of vulnerability—for example, if they lost their job or need a new car. "They are encouraged to find people's weak points," she says, showing me an advisory document for recruiters that says that, when speaking to potential recruits, you should "Focus on their WHY." It goes on to explain that you should "Spend plenty of time on this. Try to get them to connect—If you can make them cry, you have found their WHY!"

The gendered nature of MLM also provides some clues to its logic: the Direct Selling Association put the proportion of female salespeople at 73.5% in 2017, and a glance at the brands reveals that the products are largely female-oriented. Traditionally, women have different types of social networks than men, ones that lend themselves to this domestic, conversational, intimate way of selling. "Anyone worth recruitment will see joining you in this business as a relationship," says one rep on *The Dream*. As well as cashing in on this social capital, MLM businesses recognize that women are more likely to be comfortable letting a female salesperson into their home.

In return, for many women with small children, the prospect of working from home and setting your own hours is an attractive way to balance work and domestic responsibilities. "They market very heavily to highly religious communities and places where escape is not an option—for example, to military spouses and those who live on military bases," Marie says, pointing out that many of these companies proudly brand and market themselves as Christian businesses. "They praise women for

their sacrifices and talk about the virtues of motherhood—it's quite predatory and almost like grooming in that way."

There are financial reasons for the focus on women, too: for example, while women tend not to be the primary breadwinners, they do often control the household finances, which means losses are less likely to be noticed. On her podcast, Marie was told about a sort-of joke in some circles called the "husband unaware plan." "A lot of these companies actually talked about that pretty openly—like, 'Don't tell your husband how much money you're putting into it. As long as he doesn't know how much money you're spending on it, it's fine.'"

If these networks are such a bad bet that it's an open joke that participants should disguise their expenditures, why do people remain in them? Martin's theory is that it's similar to an abusive relationship that encourages secrecy and isolation, while promising something better. "You're told things like that your husband, friends and family won't understand and that if your circle isn't supportive, you should get a new one. Simultaneously you're love-bombed by your network, who are described as your 'sisters' and 'family.'"

Then there are the psychological traps that keep us all chained to bad decisions. "Some people avoid thinking about their losses and will continue participating in behavior that contributes to even more loss, out of denial and refusal to go through the pain of saying, 'I screwed up,'" Marie says. And the sunk cost fallacy also comes into play. "When you've invested so much money in something, you might as well continue—if you quit now, you're definitely out the $3,000 but if you keep going there's a chance you will make $3,001."

In the first episode of *The Dream*, Jane Marie traces the ideology behind MLM and pyramid schemes back to the human potential movement of the 1960s—a philosophy that has con-

tinued to be propagated by self-help books such as the phenomenally popular *The Secret* (2006). The contention is that we have a vast amount of untapped potential within us and unlocking it relies largely on changing the way we think and behave: Positive thinking, confidence and good behavior can lead to personal happiness and prosperity, as well as to the success of society at large. Speaking on the podcast, Pyramid Scheme Alert's Robert FitzPatrick points out that this is a foundational concept in the United States. "Thinking correctly in America is supposed to lead to prosperity," he says, describing a vision in which "there's enough for everyone; scarcity is an illusion."

These utopian ideas tug at both our sense of greed and ambition and our need to believe that things can get better for all of us. MLM makes sense at a time when political certainties are melting away and inequality is skyrocketing. While financial worries are rife for the majority, there's a small minority swimming in wealth—a minority that has no incentive to encourage others to seek equality at their expense. Everywhere, hoaxes that play on our insecurity and loss of control are thriving.

It's perhaps not a coincidence that MLM has infiltrated the highest levels of society. Between 2009 and 2011 Donald Trump himself endorsed a multi-level marketing company called The Trump Network, which sold vitamins and health products, and his education secretary Betsy DeVos' father-in-law is the co-founder of Amway, which had sales of $8.8 billion in 2018. From the kitchen table to the highest levels of government, we live in an age of false promises. And, as with nationalistic promises to restore pride and control, statistics, evidence and expertise seem powerless to cut through the kind of simple, emotional and inspiring message that MLMs present: that you are the master of your own destiny and that we can dream of better times. Aren't we all looking for that?

Pop Drip

The ritual of getting clean can get very messy.

Splash

Photography by Linus Morales & Set Design by Pernilla Löfberg

Art Direction: Erik Rödstam, Hair: Jacob Kajrup, Makeup: Marina Andersson

Left: Hair mousse by Mr. Smith. Right: Shampoo by Mr. Smith.

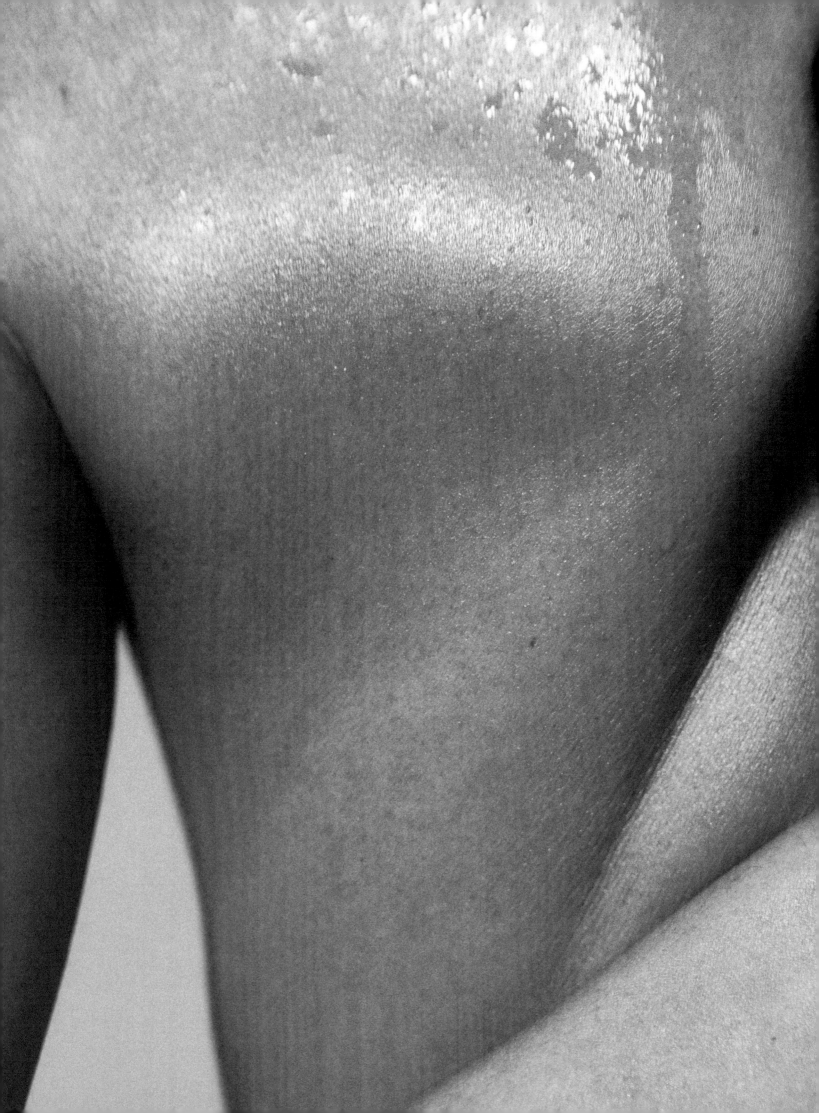

Body Oil by Herbivore Citrine.

EXCERPT:
De Cotiis Residence

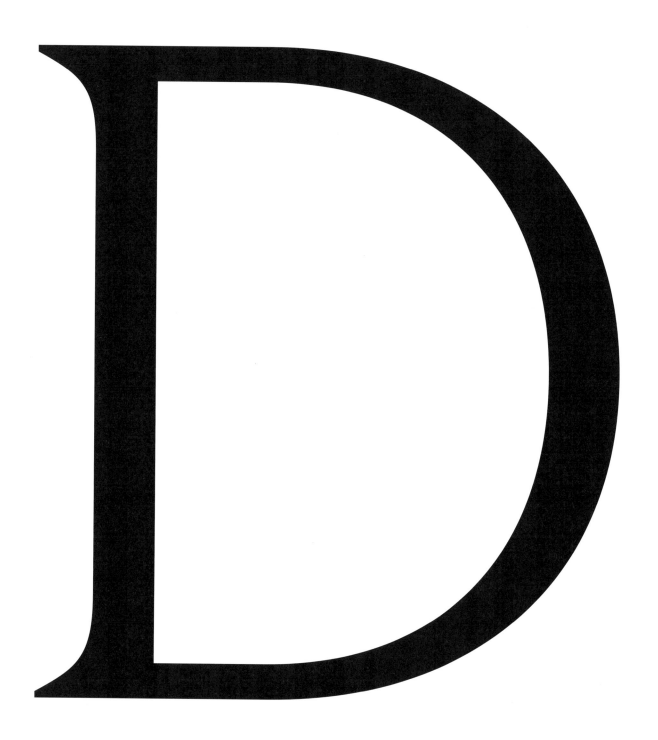

In a preview from *The Touch*—the new book from *Kinfolk* and Norm Architects, published by Gestalten—designer *Vincenzo de Cotiis* makes the case for not meddling with raw beauty: His 18th-century Milanese home is an homage to his fascination with ageing objects. Words by *Gabriele Dellisanti* & Photography by *Christian Møller Andersen*

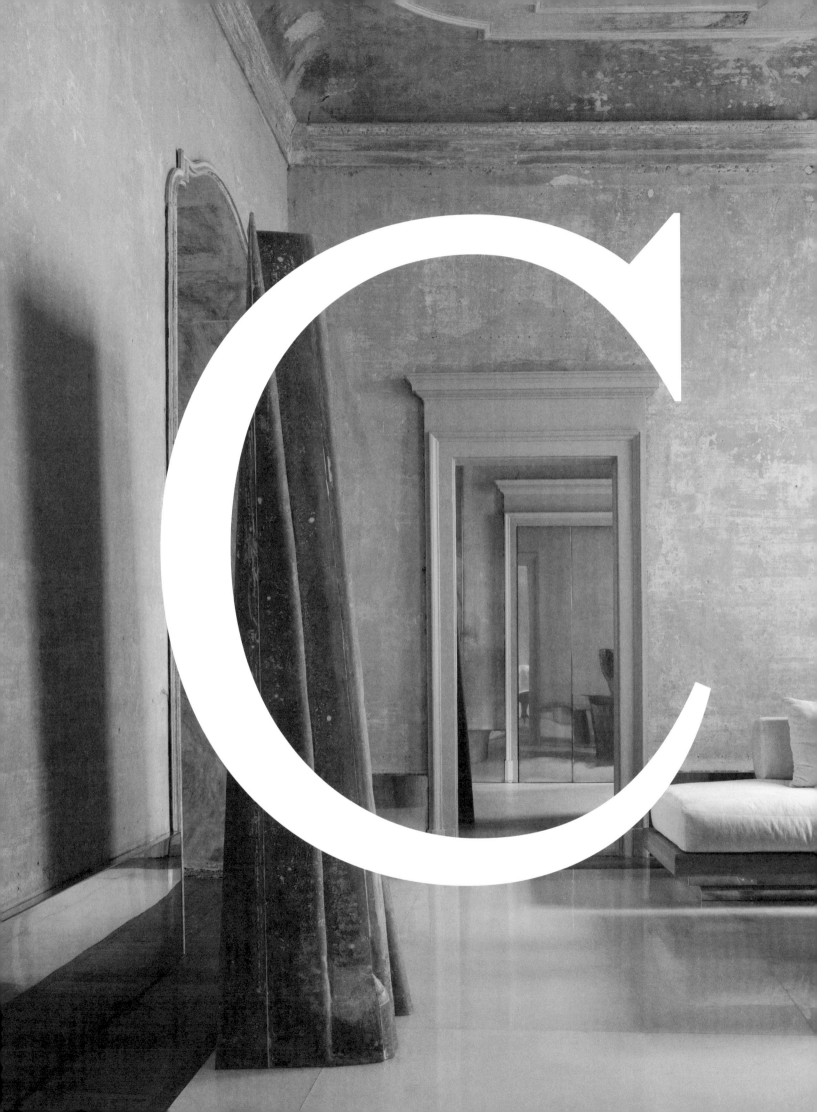

On taking over the first floor of a once-abandoned 18th-century palazzo in the Corso Magenta district of Milan, local architect and designer Vincenzo de Cotiis decided to make no structural changes to the 300-square-meter space.

Instead, he wiped the apartment of any decorative embellishments added by the families that had previously lived there, and stripped back the building's layers until he was left with only its raw antiquity. "We spent a lot of time carefully peeling away what had been added by previous owners: years of paint and paper, false ceilings, moquette floor coverings," says De Cotiis. "What was beneath—in a wonderfully imperfect, worn state—was far more incredible."

De Cotiis, who had long harbored a personal passion for time-worn objects, purposely left the apartment's crumbling walls untreated, and uncovered each room's original color scheme; the pink frescos of the library, the embellished greys and greens of the living room ceiling, and the dark green and pink Brazilian marble fixtures in the master bathroom. To this day, the walls—which are never of an entirely uniform tone—still dust those who brush against them with small fragments of plaster.

De Cotiis then furnished his home's bright and spacious rooms with many of his own sculptural creations—all of which were

De Cotiis has termed his approach "anti-design": Although his objects retain a practical functionality, he hopes that they also come to transcend it, and take on a new life as works of art.

produced in ateliers in Italy and previously showcased in a gallery space in Milan. The sculptures embody De Cotiis's constant pursuit for what he defines as "perfect imperfection."

All pieces spread across the apartment—including a long dining table crafted from silver-plated brass and recycled fiberglass, a daybed covered in hand-dyed pale pink mohair velvet, and two oddly shaped marble and cast brass coffee tables—introduce the designer's unique take on the use of reclaimed sources, and are all marked by his taste for highly tactile surfaces and deformed shapes. De Cotiis describes his style as "eclectic"; a combination of antique and futuristic elements, with materials marked by aged patinas or imperfect finishes. It is also mercurial: because of his easy access to beautiful objects, De Cotiis is frequently re-curates the apartment with new items for display.

When asked to choose his favorite room, he picks the bedroom—an intimate space which he believes encapsulates the essence of his style. Here, the apartment's original and unpolished ceiling finishes and large wooden window shutters are paired with a low platform bed and a smooth, off-white leather chair, designed by De Cotiis himself. "I prefer to emphasize the pre-existing and then enrich it," he explains.

The apartment is located inside an 18th-century Milanese townhouse with a Baroque-era landing outside.

SCRATCH THE SURFACE

by Harriet Fitch Little

De Cotiis' furniture collection is inspired by the "en plein air" tradition of the French impressionists, who set up easels in nature and made a point of trying to capture the fleeting effects of weather and season on canvas. For De Cotiis, this means honoring the natural patination of every recycled material he uses—from fiberglass to brass—in order to create objects in which imperfection becomes a signifier of luxury. (Top: DC1806. Center: DC1818. Bottom: DC1816.)

De Cotiis peeled back layers of paint in order to rediscover an authenticity that centuries of meddling had obscured.

Kaytra

Words by Sean Michaels & Photography by Ted Belton

Kaytranada built his reputation as a producer from a bedroom in his mom's house in Montreal.

Now, the whole world's his stage, but he doesn't always feel like dancing.

nada

Kaytranada's working on it. The Haitian-born, Quebec-raised producer, whose 2016 debut 99.9% was a glitter-bomb dropped onto the dance floor, is back on his grind, mixing songs, building grooves and grappling with a surprising degree of self-doubt. The last time he was doing this—finishing an album—he was living with his mom and best known as a bedroom beatmaker who put out (illicit) remixes of Janet Jackson and Missy Elliott. Since then Louis Kevin Celestin has left home, come out, and crisscrossed the planet to work with artists including Craig David and Kendrick Lamar. He's got a boyfriend now, and received Canada's most important music award—the Polaris Prize. But as much as he's living his new, best life—and that includes finding comfort in Quebec's subzero winters ("The snow puts me in a mindset of ease," he says)—the soft-spoken DJ reveals that the work hasn't gotten any easier.

SM: *Creating music must feel so different now, after all your success. You were still living at home when you released your first album.* **K:** When I think about it now, it's so weird. All I had [then] was my laptop. I wasn't even traveling to have sessions—I did just one track in studio, when I had some free time in London. Otherwise, I remember doing it in my bedroom. I remember doing it in the living room. Now it's a whole different process.

SM: *Is it just the technical side that has changed?* **K:** How can I say it? I feel like the fire, the momentum I had is not there [now]. People don't want to quite get into the ride and be on the second album. It's more difficult. When I dropped 99.9%, things went crazy. People were talking about me, my name would come up a lot. But that was what, three years ago? Now I feel like I have to prove myself again. People think, "Oh, Kaytranada—I remember him." People don't think you've [still] got it, or they don't understand the evolution of my beat-making. Everything I did with 99.9% was really stuff that I did when I was 19 or 20 years old—and now I'm 26.

SM: *It's hard to believe people's memories are that short.* **K:** I have to have a salesman mentality. To be like, "Yo, it would be cool if you got on this track. It would be revolutionary, some new shit for the game." But some people don't want to do that. Some people just want the usual, basic stuff they're comfortable with. You have to work to push them out of their comfort zone—[adopting] the producer mentality, telling them what you really need.

Kaytranada wears a bomber jacket by Andrew Szewczyk. Previous: He wears a hoodie by Andrew Szewczyk.

Growing up in Montreal, Kaytranada was influenced by his parents listening to kompa—Haitian dance music—but opted for hip-hop when he had control of the stereo.

Finding success while still a teen meant that Kaytranada never finished high school.

"I feel like I have to prove myself again. People don't think you've still got it."

SM: *So has your sound changed?* **K:** I've always been influenced by disco, but I'm taking that more seriously and bringing that theme to the album—this feel-good, club kind of music: love songs that are danceable, breakup songs that are danceable. Music for DJs. Up-tempo, drum-break stuff, an '80s hip-hop [vibe]. A lot of Afrobeat influence, a lot of dancehall influence. A mixture of everything. But I feel like that mixture is myself, you know? Whenever I make a beat, it's going to sound like me.

SM: *How do you build a track? Do you have an idea in your head—a feeling, a concept, some kind of musical image?* **K:** It's more freestyle. I'll start with a high hat and build around it, add the kick drums and the bass line—singing to myself until I find something I feel in my gut. It never quite comes out like what I had in my head, but it sounds hot anyway. And then I add the chords, or the [vocals]… The easiest way to make beats used to be sampling, but the sampling game is dying right now.

SM: *Do you stick around for the winter in Montreal? It's hard for me to imagine you making such sunny music here.* **K:** Last year I escaped for two months maybe, but I actually kind of enjoy it. The snow puts me in a mindset of ease. I'm in a condo, I don't need to do the hard work outside. Watching white snow [falling] outside, seeing how white it is, it's like, "OK, I can chill." I don't have to do anything besides make beats.

SM: *Can you tell when you've made something really good? Or do you have wait until you've played it for somebody else?* **K:** I used to know. Now, because I've been so much in my own head, I'm not as sure. I'll show it to my manager, but I can tell when he's faking it. Sometimes he'll just say, "That's sick," and that's it—and you know that it's not as crazy [as it should be]. But when I show him something that's full of energy, he'll be like, "Yo those drums, man! Those drums you added!" He'll be really

specific—and then you can tell. When people really like something, it's in their face.

SM: *Do you dance to your own stuff?* **K:** Totally. If you see me live in my DJ sets, sometimes I'm the only one dancing in the whole room. And when I make beats, I'll bob my head so hard. That's when I know, "This one is ready to go."

SM: *Are you happiest when you're just starting a new song? Or when it's finished?* **K:** When it's done. It's like: "One song down, boom." My people are finally going to hear it, and stop complaining.

SM: *Who's complaining?* **K:** You get tweets. "We're waiting for a damn album, what the fuck Kaytranada?" Or Instagram DMs: "Could we get an album, sir, please?" But y'all don't understand—it's difficult. As a producer, making an album, trying to keep linked with everybody, especially not living in LA—it's so difficult, man. I know I'm a strong motherfucker and one day [the album] will come out, no matter what, but it drives me crazy sometimes.

SM: *Knowing that—that it will eventually come out, and people will love it—isn't that a comfort?* **K:** I feel like I have two people inside of me. One of them always says, "Yeah, don't worry about it." And then the other [part of me] is like, "Oh goddamn—ain't you worried about your album?" [My friends say] "Don't worry. You don't need to worry at all. Take your damn time." And they're right. If D'Angelo can take 10 years to drop an album, if André 3000's not dropping an album—I shouldn't worry about it, honestly. But I feel like I have to. When I drop the second album I want everybody to know, right away, "That's a Kaytranada joint." If somebody doesn't know me—when they hear a song and ask, "Oh, what is that?" [I want] everyone [else] to be like: "Yeah. That's Kaytra."

The Big

The best parties have no invite list, and definitely no last orders.

Swing

Photography by Luc Braquet & Styling by Camille-Joséphine Teisseire

Previous: Katya wears a shirt by Sandro, a skirt by Dior and shoes by Repetto. Nataliya wears a dress by Fifi Chachnil, earrings by Noguchi at White Bird, a bracelet by Sophie Bille Brahe at White Bird and shoes by Hermès. Above Left: Katya wears a dress by Balmain and earrings by Annette Ferdinandsen at White Bird. Victorien wears a polo shirt by Hermès and trousers by Dior. Above Right: Victorien wears a suit by Dior, a turtleneck by COS and a beret by Stetson. Right: Nataliya wears a dress by Sandro, vintage earrings, a ring by Oona at White Bird and shoes by Dior.

Above: Katya wears a dress by Emporio Armani. Victorien wears a jacket by Vivienne Westwood. Right: Katya wears a top by Fifi Chachnil and a necklace by Chanel Joaillerie. Nataliya wears a dress by Sandro and vintage earrings. Anaïs wears a shirt by Vivienne Westwood and pants by Rochas. Victorien wears a shirt by Rochas and a bowtie by Charvet.

Left: Nataliya wears a dress by Rochas, vintage earrings, a scarf by Koché and shoes by Dior. Above Left: Victorien wears a shirt by Off-White and trousers and a tie by Hermès. Above Right: Katya wears a body suit by Dior, trousers by See by Chloé, a headscarf by Laurence Bossion, earrings by Annette Ferdinandsen at White Bird, a belt by Hermès and a pearl necklace by Chanel Joaillerie.

Archive:
Roberto
Burle Marx

Buoyed by the bossa nova experimentalism of mid-century Brazil, an opera-loving landscape architect struck out against the diktats of cool modernism. Words by *Cody Delistraty*

For Le Corbusier, the rainforests of South America reminded him of "the horrible mold" that would collect in and around his mother's homemade jars of jam. The open expanse of the Amazon struck the famed modernist with, if not fear exactly, then at least a great deal of frustration. With tropics and wildlife, the impulse to control was futile.

For the Brazilian designer Roberto Burle Marx, however, who was studying European modernism in Berlin while Le Corbusier was flying over the Amazon, the tropics were not an intractable "mold" but instead represented the possibility of rethinking design's relationship to nature altogether. What if, instead of the kind of concrete-poured control that Le Corbusier insisted upon, landscape design might be integrated within its surroundings? Burle Marx's best-known work—an undulating design of white, black and brown paving stones along the Copacabana boardwalk in Rio de Janeiro—illustrates his drive to activate landscapes, rather than prescribe them.

Burle Marx grew up in early 20th-century Brazil, a time defined as much by the incoming military dictatorship as by a growing environmental consciousness, bossa nova music and burgeoning artistic liberalism. He was born in 1909 in São Paulo to an upwardly mobile Jewish immigrant father and a Catholic mother, who was a talented gardener. His parents were particularly cosmopolitan: The writer Stefan Zweig and the composer Heitor Villa-Lobos dropped by their spacious home from time to time, and the pianist Arthur Rubinstein stayed with them whenever he had concerts in the area. As a teenager, Burle Marx studied opera in São Paolo. When he turned 19, he left to study painting in Berlin. His parents tagged along, taking him away from his studies three, four, sometimes five nights a week in order to go to the opera, with particular emphasis on those by Wagner and Strauss.

"There was almost nothing, in any aspect of culture, that Burle Marx wasn't a part of," says Edward J. Sullivan, a professor of art history at NYU, who specializes in Latin American art and is curator of the Burle Marx retrospective that opened at the New York Botanical Garden in June 2019. "He was a Renaissance man and somebody who excelled at virtually everything he did."

In Berlin, he established his design basis in modernism with numerous trips to see paintings by Picasso and Van Gogh. A presentation of exotic Brazilian plants at the Berlin-Dahlem Botanical Garden, arranged in a European style, had a particular effect on him. The philodendrons, water lilies and snakewood plants—all common in Brazil but generally ignored in Brazilian gardening practices—were here lovingly organized and showcased, unlocking in Burle Marx a desire to rethink the immense floral resources he had access to back home.

"His goal was to use his gardens' design not to control—but to unlock."

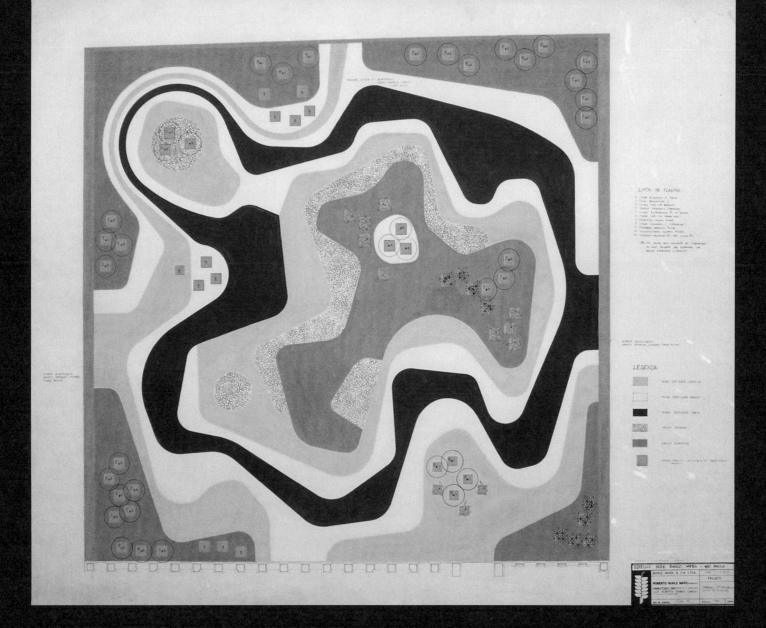

Above: Design for the Safra Bank,
Head Office Building, São Paulo.
Gouache on paper. © Burle Marx
Landscape Design Studio.

"There was almost nothing that Burle Marx wasn't a part of. He was a Renaissance man."

"It was there that I realized the strength of the pristine nature of the tropics, that I had there, in my hands, as raw matter ready to serve to my own artistic project," he recalled in a conference he gave in 1954. His career moved rapidly. He returned to Brazil, studied painting at the National School of Fine Arts in Rio, and received a commission from Lúcio Costa—an architect and urban designer and one of his professors—to design a private garden. Two years later, Burle Marx was directing the planning of all urban parks in Recife, in the country's northeast, before striking out on his own, eventually designing over 3,000 gardens around the world.

One of the most important buildings he helped design was Rio's 15-story Ministry of Education and Health, also called the Gustavo Capanema Palace. Designed between 1935 and 1936, it became the first public building in the Americas to be designed using modernist principles.

Lúcio Costa and Oscar Niemeyer asked Le Corbusier to advise on the project, and the building's raised pillars—about 10 feet high to allow for unobstructed access—show the French architect's influence, as does the structural airiness of its facade. But the building also stands as one of the great Brazilian architectural accomplishments thanks to Burle Marx's gardens. The floor tiles and murals were designed under his direction, creating artworks and color schemes that "cannibalized" European modernist culture while also defying it, as the poet Oswald de Andrade had implored Brazilian artists to do in his 1928 *Manifesto Antropófago*. Burle Marx's tropical gardens make up the courtyard and contain rare plant life, including the *Roystonea oleracea*, a kind of palm tree found only in Latin America. He also designed the roof garden, relying again on the typical Brazilian plant life that had captivated him in Berlin decades before. The building's architectural style underscored the enormous gulf between Brazil's official authoritarian politics and the open, democratic ideals valued by Burle Marx. It was commissioned during the reign of Getúlio Vargas—the dictator who ruled for 15 years and modeled much of his public image after Benito Mussolini and the

Italian fascists. But Burle Marx's winding garden paths and his reorganization of plants based on painterly principles (grouped often by color, as though pigments on a canvas) marked Brazil's mid-century cultural liberation and antiauthoritarian impulses. The gardens literally led to nowhere. They were solely about beauty rather than commerce or military might. Burle Marx was never an outright government protestor. He worked with the military council but believed that he could shape Brazil's cultural policies from the inside out. He needed a platform to affect preservation and climate change.

"He worked with the government while also making speeches about the destruction of the Amazon, about the environmental perils that his own gardens faced," said Sullivan. "Ultimately, this made him one of the most important figures in the fight to preserve nature in Brazil."

Burle Marx's style of landscape architecture is situated within the broader category of modernist architecture, but he always believed that a designer must be proficient in the entirety of his style, ideally the whole of art history, not just a single niche. His goal was to use his gardens' design not to control—but to unlock. Observe his former home in Rio, lush with nearly 500 plant varietals, or walk down the 2½-mile promenade that he designed along Copacabana Beach, and one finds that his detailed attention leads to design that is not oppressive but freeing; a bossa nova energy carries you as you stroll along the seaside.

Burle Marx died in Rio in 1994. Today, under President Jair Bolsonaro, Brazil is facing the threat of environmental degradation like never before. Is there an artist who will step up now, to wield the language of political activism while also introducing a fresh form of design?

"That's what I hope more than anything to achieve with this exhibition," Sullivan says of his show. "We want to not only bring the personality of Burle Marx to the fore but also to show how one can speak the design language of preservation when, today, there's a huge danger to Brazilian—and global—nature."

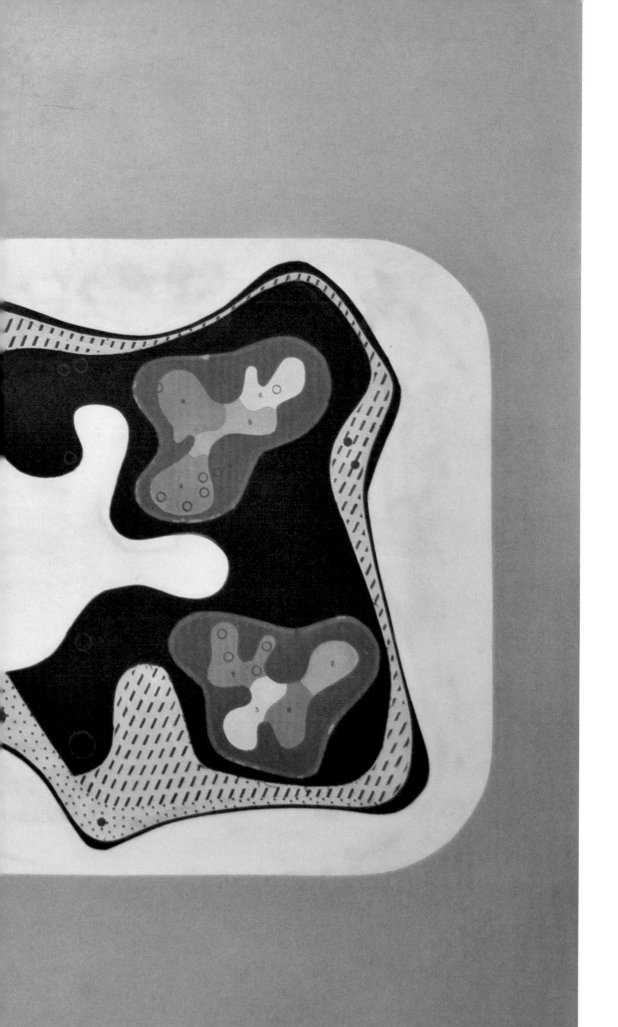

Burle Marx's design for the Largo do Machado Square in Rio de Janeiro. Automotive painting over woodboard. © Burle Marx Landscape Design Studio.

3
Education

Erica Chi

Photography by Justin Chung & Styling by Jesse Arifien

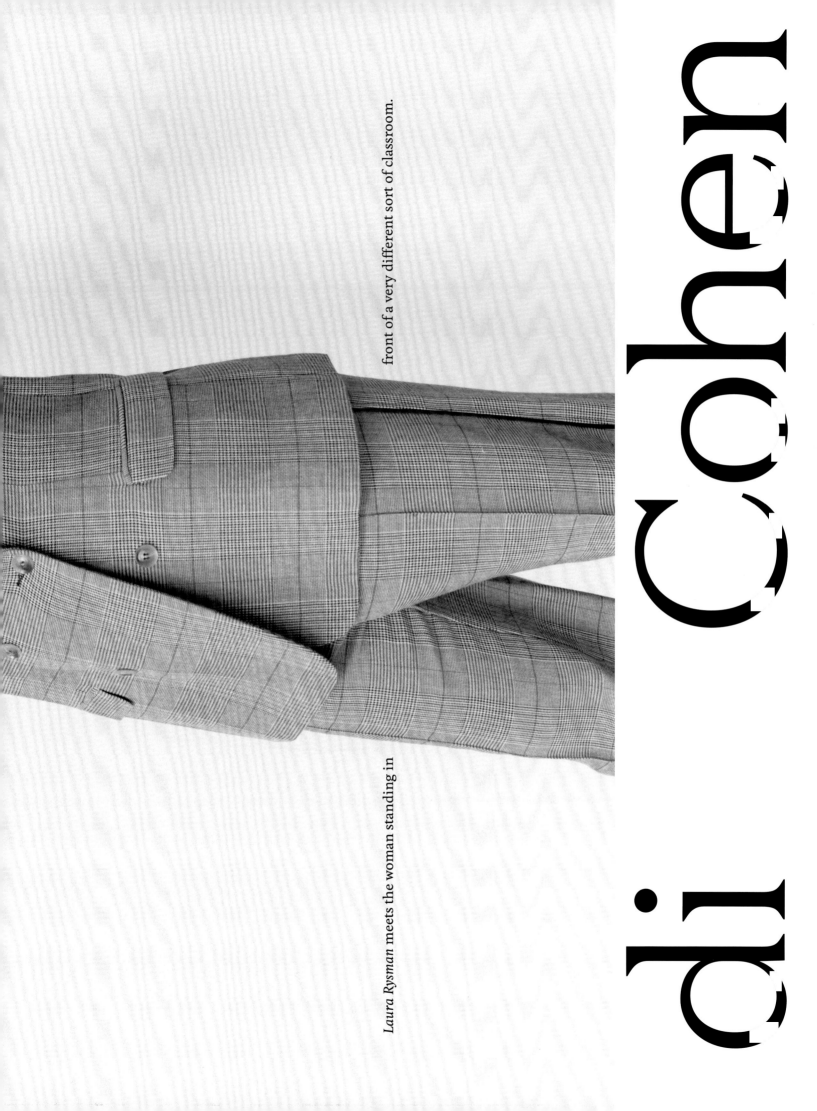

di

Cohen

Laura Rysman meets the woman standing in front of a very different sort of classroom.

The sanctuary-like Los Angeles headquarters of Loom—a bright white box with sun-filled and soft-hued interiors—stands distinct from the surrounding single-story strip of drab, Mid-City commercial sprawl. It is a visibly fresh beacon extolling a new approach to sex, bodies and healthcare. A community and education center that opened in 2018, Loom is a for-profit enterprise, but its mission feels downright political in the face of America's current rights-limiting legislation and an increasingly negligent medical system.

"The body is political and how we're able to understand it has a political component," says Erica Chidi Cohen, the 32-year-old CEO of Loom who founded the company with Quinn Lundberg. "When people have body literacy and can advocate for themselves, they have better health outcomes. That's what women and people of color need." She speaks to me from across the planet, beamed from Los Angeles into my home in Tuscany nine time zones away but, forthright and self-possessed, Chidi Cohen is immediate enough that I feel I'm being schooled. I sit up straight.

Chidi Cohen is Loom's principal teacher, creating a curriculum that's reviewed for scientific accuracy by a community of ob-gyns and medical professionals, and informed by her 10 years working with women's health. It's information that's fact-based, but which evangelizes a new attitude. The author of *Nurture: A Modern Guide to Pregnancy, Birth, Early Motherhood—and Trusting Yourself and Your Body*, and the creator of the *Nurture* online birth course, Chidi Cohen's experience began when she became a doula and a founding member of the Birth Justice Project to help incarcerated women in San Francisco. "I liked that being a doula was more of an educational and emotional role, and not as focused on the clinical components of pregnancy and labor," she says, sitting at her home desk in a ribbed black tank dress and twisted gold chains, her bob of skinny locks bouncing as she munches on sliced cantaloupe. "The core skills of a doula are in educating people about their options," she says. It's a notion she's developed into a full-scale teaching center with Loom, where she's amplified her call for an empowered, egalitarian approach to women and their bodies.

"Education is so important because healthcare is letting women down," she says. Chidi Cohen thinks that our abbreviated medical visits inhibit open communication between doctors and patients. "And healthcare is not universal in the US, so who you get to see and what's

Previous: Erica wears a suit by Bassike and shoes by COS. Left: She wears a shirt by Rachel Comey and trousers by ALC. Right: She wears a blouse by Sylvia Tcherassi, trousers by COS, earrings by Rachel Comey and her own rings.

Hair & Makeup: Nicole Wittman

available to you depends on your socioeconomic situation. If we can't get people healthcare, we need to get them education so they can get the best from what they're going to encounter."

On May 21 this year, in response to anti-abortion regulations in 13 states, Loom joined six other female-led companies (Sustain, THINX, Dame, Cora, Clara Collection and Fur) to run a full-page ad in *The New York Times* proclaiming a woman's right to choose, and the business community's responsibility to support that right. "With the rollback of access, it was important to get ahead of it and make people understand that abortion is healthcare. It's a human rights issue," says Chidi Cohen. "As a black queer person, I really feel that the personal is political." Within its scope of offerings, Loom provides abortion support groups and connects women with abortion doulas. "We see it as part of the reproductive continuum, so it felt right to put the business in front of this issue. The reason that it's even an issue is that there's so little respect for women, and a deep desire to control and restrict women."

Chidi Cohen is vigilant about shifting semantics as well, rejecting common nomenclature like "natural birth," with its implication of a superior childbearing route, and "PMS," with its historical denigration of a woman at the whim of her hormones. "We're moving away from paternal terms," she says, as Nima, her darkly marbled Manx cat, jumps onto the desk. Chidi Cohen caresses him without breaking the flow of her thoughts: that new terminology, new ways of speaking about rote subjects help her open up new ways of thinking. "Health education requires a lot more poetry in terms of looseness with language," she says.

Loom classes introduce a new vocabulary (an example that she insists upon: "feeling luteal"—a reference to the post-ovulation phase of a woman's cycle—replaces "PMSing"). The space also fosters a frank, conversation-based style of instruction that comes easily to Chidi Cohen and galvanizes her participants. "People self-select when they decide to be in a class as adults," she points out. No one is there who doesn't want to be there, who isn't hoping to be inspired to participate in discussions. "My job as an educator is really to help create a container in the room where everyone feels the conversation is guided," she says. Chidi Cohen freely shares personal stories to let her students know "that I'm human and going through my own experience," talking about her own body, sex and her partnership with her husband, lawyer Jordy Cohen.

"What would it look like to have a matriarchal academia and work culture?"

Left: Erica wears a coat by COS and her own rings. Above: She wears a coat by COS.

Her upbringing, split between South Africa and the United States, was guided by parents who were both clinicians—her father an endocrinologist, her mother a nurse. It was a household that encouraged "talking about the body and talking about fluids," she says. Perhaps not coincidentally, she found out from her father that her grandmother and great-grandmother in Nigeria were both midwives.

For the sex class at Loom, Chidi Cohen rounds out her discussions with prompts. In the beginning: What's a single word to describe how you feel about sex? And by the conclusion, when things have grown more comfortably provocative: What's one thing you think you're really good at when it comes to sex? In between, she instills what she calls "an antidote to hot sex-partner performance." This is not *Cosmo*. This is not about 10 tricks that will drive your lover wild. This is a class "about helping people understand that their primary sexual relationship is with themselves," says Chidi Cohen, ignoring Nima as he nuzzles her neck from the desktop. "How can you know yourself better? How can you feel more anchored in what turns you on and what doesn't?"

Much of it comes from modeling the behavior for students, she says, which means discussing how she takes pleasure for herself. A student once asked if masturbating on her stomach was abnormal, to which Chidi Cohen replied reassuringly that she'd also done it, and then others in the class concurred. She went on to explain that many women begin masturbating that way in order to put pressure on their vestibular bulbs, which rub against the clitoris—the clitoris being not just the hooded, pea-size glans, as many believe, but a much larger, wishbone-shaped network of erectile tissue that extends deep into the vagina. Desire, meet edification.

The class's curriculum promotes a startlingly clear picture of anatomy alongside how to unabashedly ask for and receive pleasure. In *The History of Sexuality*, Michel Foucault famously criticized Western society for its obsession with *scientia sexualis*—a sterile and confessional science of sex, or "procedures for telling the truth of sex which are geared to a form of knowledge-power strictly opposed to the art of initiations

Left: Erica wears a turtleneck and coat by COS. Right: She wears a sweater by Bassike. Left: Erica wears a turtleneck and coat by COS. Right: She wears a sweater by Bassike.

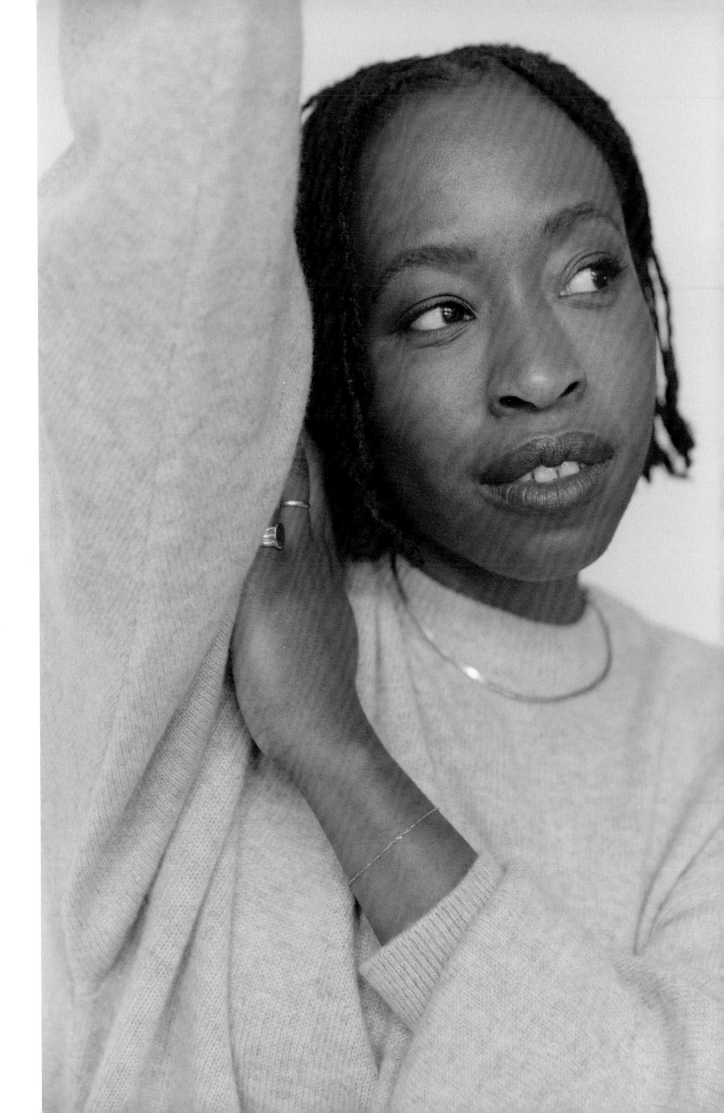

Below: Erica wears a coat, trousers and shoes by COS. Right: She wears a suit by Bassike.

> *"Our culture is not permissive of being anything else than 100 percent optimal. Women need elasticity."*

and the masterful secret." He criticized the lack of *ars erotica*, an esoteric erotic art where pleasure is considered "[not] by reference to a criterion of utility, but first and foremost in relation to itself." But Chidi Cohen considers her work to be simultaneously revealing the antiseptic, scientific truths of sex and its voluptuous, often censored codes. "I like to mix the two," she says. "All of those things need to speak to each other: science, anatomy and the emotion of pleasure. A scientific framework can give you permission that you wouldn't give yourself."

Other Loom classes equally endeavor to shake off convention. "What makes our pregnancy classes popular and revolutionary is that we're not necessarily creating a hierarchy around birth," says Chidi Cohen. All childbearing options are equal and presented in detail. "One of the most feminist decisions you can make is to decide how you want to feel in labor," she says. (Loom students are majority female, but men join in the pregnancy class to support their partners, and attend the parenting class as well.)

The course on periods, functioning "like cognitive behavioral therapy," says Chidi Cohen, is "an invitation to reimagine your relationship with your menstrual cycle." Designed to shift the menstruation paradigm to incorporate awareness of the entire month-long hormonal cycle ("bleed to bleed," Chidi Cohen calls it), the class mitigates the shame and stress most women have at some point associated with their period in favor of openness, with a biological and emotional comprehension of what's happening to the body. "Who you are in your pre-ovulatory phase and who you are in your post-ovulatory phase are very different. That's what's in your hormones," Chidi Cohen explains. I make note

and silently pledge to start paying attention to this previously ignored personal calendar of hormonal changes.

"Our culture is not permissive of being anything else than 100 percent optimal at all times, but women need elasticity," she says. "It's not normal for women to feel 100 percent all the time." Phrased in less upbeat language, this is a sentiment that I had long shuddered at, and that men have not infrequently used to justify the exclusion of women from positions as top professionals. I'm just 10 years older than Chidi Cohen, but the feminism I was reared on glowered at any mention of hormonal vulnerability. We were taught to be steel. We were taught to be men. Yet despite the retrograde misogyny on full view in the current political arena, women have gained a decade of ground, and there's more hard-won space for female reality today, some of it being undoubtedly cemented by projects like Loom and the voices it encourages.

The conversation among women like Chidi Cohen is no longer about taking over the system but recasting the system entirely. "To be a successful woman has meant divorce from the body," she tells me. "The roles were designed around the patriarchy, and men don't have the same hormonal variability. Things aren't set up to support the matriarchy." Nima paws her shoulder, looking for attention, but Chidi Cohen will not be distracted. "How do we get cisgender men to gatekeep this info and understand its importance? How do we rebuild environments to absorb our normal functions?" she asks, her eyes widening in earnestness as she nudges the cat to the side. "What would it look like to have a matriarchal academia and a matriarchal work culture?" A revolution is brewing. I hope I get to see it too.

Hair & Makeup: Josephine Mai

Free

One hour to unwind, refresh and reenergize before bouncing back into the day.

Period

Photography by Romain Laprade & Styling by Camille-Joséphine Teisseire

Above: Wilbert wears a suit by Givenchy, a gilet by Eric Bompard and a shirt by Sandro. Right: He wears a polo shirt by De Fursac, vintage Adidas shorts and a cap by Holiday Boileau.

Above: Wilbert wears a shirt by Sandro, trousers by Paul Smith, a belt by Hermès, socks by Falke and moccasins by J.M. Weston. Right: He wears a top by Holiday Boileau, vintage Adidas shorts, socks by Falke and sneakers by AMI.

Above: Wilbert takes off a T-shirt by Sandro. Right: He wears a top by Holiday Boileau and vintage leather shorts.

Above: Wilbert wears a top by Sandro, shorts by Adidas x Alexander Wang, socks by Holiday Boileau and sneakers by AMI. Right: He wears a sweater by Octobre Edition and trousers by Hugo Boss.

THE RISE
OF THE FREE-RANGE
CLASSROOM

TEXT:
DAPHNÉE DENIS

Traditional schools were created in the image of factory lines. Now, an increasing number of parents and educators are asking whether a system that prioritizes good results and blind obedience is the best fit for a generation of free thinkers. Daphnée Denis gets to grips with the idea of opting out—from a Japanese nursery with no walls to a Parisian high school with no grades.

"All in all, you're just another brick in the wall." Pink Floyd's rock opera *The Wall*—a protest hymn against education—comes to mind when looking at Tokyo's Fuji Kindergarten. The Montessori preschool is so far removed from the traditional school system that its architect, Takaharu Tezuka, decided to completely do away with the object of Pink Floyd's wrath: The building has no walls. Children aged two to six roam free in the ring-shaped building, where sliding doors open on to a central outside playground. Classrooms are separated by wooden boxes originally intended as shelves but often used for children's play instead. It can get loud, but that's part of the design: The children are meant to concentrate through the white noise of surrounding classes. Trees grow inside the building and through the rooftop, which doubles as a circular track where kids chase each other, climb on branches and run endless laps. "If the boy in the corner doesn't want to stay in the room, we let him go. He will come back eventually, because it's a circle," Tezuka explains in a TED Talk about Fuji.

The preschool, built in 2007, has won many design awards. It's a building that reflects its philosophy: Children shouldn't have to sit quietly listening to a teacher for hours on end, they should be granted more independence and learn by discovering things on their own.

This is not a novel idea: Progressive pedagogies like Montessori and Waldorf-Steiner have been around for over a hundred years. And yet most public education systems around the world continue to offer traditional schools with closed classrooms divided by age groups, where the pupils face their teachers in silence, take notes, memorize facts and must pass exams in order to be promoted into the following grade.

To understand why some people opt out of the traditional system, it is helpful to look at what those schools were originally designed to do. The idea that everyone is entitled to a basic education would have seemed ludicrous before the 19th century. Historically, in the West, knowledge was controlled by the Church and imparted to men from the elite classes. With the Industrial Revolution, however, it became apparent that workers should receive some form of training to increase their productivity. A man who knew how to read, write and count became more valuable in the context of mechanized mass labor. France and Germany were the first countries to introduce state-funded mandatory schools for children, which promoted literacy through rote learning and discipline. In many ways, these new school systems were remarkable: They made it possible to educate the masses. But their goal was never to create free thinkers. In fact, as the prominent

education reformer Ken Robinson has pointed out, traditional schools were created in the image of factory lines, with ringing bells, separate facilities and subjects taught in isolation from one another. Robinson goes so far as to argue that the children are dealt with "by batches," with age groupings as a substitute for date of manufacture.

This factory-inspired, one-size-fits-all approach to schooling has clear limits. For starters, it treats children as readily exchangeable goods that should all follow the same curriculum at the same time to obtain the same results. If some pupils fail to do that, then they are considered damaged goods, and deemed less intelligent than their peers. One problem, of course, is that a child isn't an empty vessel waiting to be filled with knowledge. Another issue is that by teaching children to parrot lessons and follow orders, the system makes them more docile and suggestible. At the beginning of the 20th century, and increasingly so after the blood-drenched First World War, thinkers started questioning this model and looking for ways to use education in order to foster democracy and to encourage independence over blind obedience. "It was an age of thinking about a better way forward for society," says Christine Doddington, fellow emerita of educational philosophy at the University of Cambridge. "These early people saw education as key to what society would become. They realized childhood wasn't just a time that you went through, they started to look at the notion of childhood as being a preparation for the adult world in a way that wasn't really considered before."

In his 1916 book *Democracy and Education*, American philosopher John Dewey made the case for a child-centered approach to schooling, based on the idea that children were active learners who could make decisions on their own and should be pushed to collaborate with others in a stimulating environment. Instead of expecting children to just receive and memorize disjointed facts and hope that they piece them together later on, as fully grown citizens, Dewey argued that minors should be considered active members of society already. In that sense, even though he never endorsed her method, his observations were in line with those of another progressive educator: Maria Montessori.

The first woman to graduate from medical school at the University of Rome, Montessori approached education as a scientist. She first started working with children in asylums, as a voluntary assistant doctor at the university's psychiatric clinic. Her interest in "feeble-minded children" came after she witnessed the conditions in which they were treated: These youngsters were kept with adults, and no efforts were made to care for them beyond keeping them alive. The more she observed them, the more she believed that their problems could be addressed with education rather than medicine. After researching methods developed by other physicians for those with special needs, she obtained permission to move some of these "idiot children" into an empty hospital and started testing out her materials on them, observing what worked and refining

her teachings accordingly. Her goal was to design attractive, holistic courses, where children would have to use their senses as well as reason to understand concepts. It was a success. Many of her "defective" students learned to read and write, and managed to pass state exams.

This achievement led Montessori to wonder whether similar methods would work on typical children, too. In 1907, she founded the first "Casa dei Bambini," or "Children's Home," where she tried out her alternative academic materials on children from the slums. Like people with special needs, poor children were considered inept and few in the wider society cared whether Montessori's experiments would hurt them. Fortunately, the children flourished. Better still, Montessori made one groundbreaking discovery: Given the right guidance, they actually enjoyed learning things. Her eponymous method would eventually become world famous, and it remains influential today. Montessori schools follow a set of precepts: They favor mixed-age classes, where children help each other and decide what they want to study at any given time. Teachers don't give out grades and are discouraged from publicly praising the pupils. The school materials are self-correcting, since the children are expected to fix their mistakes on their own after checking the right answers.

Around the same time, other thinkers came up with different methods to circumvent the rigidity of state schools. In Germany, Rudolph Steiner imagined the Waldorf system, still widespread in Europe and the United States, in which children are taught in seven-year cycles with a strong focus on artistic and emotional development. Students at Waldorf schools only start working on abstract or conceptual subjects at 15, an age considered more appropriate to grasp these ideas. Meanwhile, in France, educator Célestin Freinet vowed to "throw all

"Being book smart doesn't always equal acting intelligently. Standardized tests have become a tool to benchmark people, leaving those deemed unintelligent behind."

school books overboard," resigned from his job as a public school teacher and founded his own school in Vence. His method emphasized the need for children to self-govern, and learn through cooperation on common projects.

These alternative approaches to schooling rely on some common principles. Children should learn by doing, and take the center stage when it comes to their education. Subjects like math or physics shouldn't be taught separately but rather in connection to one another, so that students grasp how to apply them in real life. Finally, schools should reject standardized testing. These methods are radically opposed to what's on offer in traditional schools, namely classes centered on a teacher imparting knowledge, separate subjects, and exams—a lot of them.

Of course, there is a reason why tests exist: to make sure that the learning is achieved, and that lessons are up to the standard set by each nation's education system. So who's wrong? "The discussion about what it is to know dates back to the Greeks," says Christine Doddington of Cambridge University. "It started to get translated into: 'Knowledge is fact, so you've got to regurgitate facts, information, and you'll be knowledgeable.' But actually, it's not just about knowing something, it's about understanding it. It's a different activity of thinking. We're not creating smart people because we're not creating thinkers, we're creating people who can regurgitate."

Because universal education systems as we know them date back to the 19th century, their design is heavily influenced by the Enlightenment's view of intelligence—which values logical thinking and knowledge of the classics. This approach has been described by American developmental psychologist Howard Gardner as "Westist, Testist and Bestist": Schools constantly try to quantify children's intellectual ability and rely on a one-dimensional view of the correct way to tackle a problem. By doing this, Gardner contends, they fail to take into account how multifaceted human intelligence is and overlook one rather important point: Being book smart doesn't always equal acting intelligently. Standardized tests have become a tool to benchmark people, leaving those deemed unintelligent behind. As French philosopher Michel Foucault famously argued: "Diplomas are made for those who don't have them."

A caricatured view of alternative pedagogies is that they let children do whatever they want, with little adult supervision. Admittedly, this was the case in some "free schools" created in the 1970s, but the vast majority of progressive schools are not teacher-free zones. "With Montessori, the children are writing reports; what changes is the expectation that these reports are graded, and that everybody should be giving the same answer," says Dr. Angeline Lillard, professor of developmental psychology at the University of Virginia. "You look for a good answer, instead of a specific one." Lillard's research focuses on how cognitive sciences have proven most of Maria Montessori's observations right. As a proponent of a radical overhaul of the state school system, she argues that the Italian physician's findings, still in use and efficient a century later, should be the preferred model for education.

Perhaps ironically, one of the main obstacles to making such a method the norm is that it isn't trademarked. There is no compulsory Montessori certification, so any school can implement it, sometimes poorly. But the real issue lies in how different alternative schools are from the typical performance-driven systems. Even though research shows that children in nontraditional schools have better mental health and obtain better results, it's still much easier to measure a child's ability to answer a multiple choice test than it is to assess individual thought. In most Western countries, education reform is heading in the opposite direction, with heavier state monitoring of teachers and students alike, and little room for more creative approaches to education. Because state-funded programs mostly shun progressive methods, alternative schools are considered a luxury, only available to the rich.

But some public school systems, like the Finnish one, are incorporating research and forward-thinking pedagogies. There are also over 500 state-funded Montessori schools in the United States, and public, grade-free high schools are slowly appearing in France. "Of course my dream is to create this kind of school in the public system," says Pascale Haag, the director of the Parisian Lab School Network, which combines on-site development research with a hybrid curriculum inspired by the Montessori, Waldorf and Steiner methods. "There's no point in creating an elitist system that cannot be transposed; we aim to work hand-in-hand with the Ministry of National Education." Although her school doesn't grade children, it does prepare them to sit national exams.

If change is possible, perhaps the question isn't why people opt out of the traditional system, but rather why most schools haven't moved on from it themselves. Society's view of the purpose of education has become more refined, yet our schools still follow an outdated model—one that educators and researchers have questioned for more than a century. "My vision of the future is no longer of people taking exams and proceeding from one grade to the next," Maria Montessori wrote in 1948, "but of individuals passing from one stage of independence to a higher one by means of their own will." The walls to bring down may well be in our minds.

Archive:
Buckminster Fuller

No work, no knowledge silos and whole weeks spent learning inside a giant geodesic dome: *Tim Hornyak* remembers a time when the future of education belonged to Buckminster Fuller.

Photograph: Courtesy of The Estate of Buckminster Fuller

In the 1960s, the architect and author Buckminster Fuller was a sensation on the university lecture circuit. Delivering over 400 talks a year in a time of social upheaval, he enchanted students with visions of how human society could provide for all at the expense of none. What we had to do, he said, was be naive and follow nature's design principles.

Fuller's legacy as an educator is inextricably linked to his architectural creations. Growing up in Montreal, I would listen to my father rhapsodize about Expo 67, a world's fair held on the Saint Lawrence River. There was a driverless monorail, Soviet satellites and luminaries including Jackie Kennedy and Maurice Chevalier. Built on natural and artificial islands, it drew nearly 50 million people and was one of the must successful world fairs ever held. Like the giant inverted pyramid that was the Canadian pavilion, Expo 67 was "a miracle," historian Pierre Berton wrote. In the 1980s I would walk through remnants of Expo 67 on Île Sainte-Hélène. Its utopian vision of the future seemed a forgotten dream but for its architectural legacy. There was the delightful jumble of Moshe Safdie's Habitat 67, the Place des Nations and pavilions repurposed into the Casino de Montreal. But the structure that captured my imagination was Fuller's geodesic dome.

Like a giant geopolitical soap bubble, the dome housed the US pavilion and faced off against the Soviet pavilion across a canal. Fuller's sphere was made of transparent acrylic sheeting wrapped over

Fuller thought that children were "de-geniusized" by mainstream education and believed in giving top marks to the ones who made the most mistakes.

steel trusses. Inside, the longest escalator ever built led to exhibits about Hollywood movies and the conquest of space. It projected American know-how, power and prestige, but it also reflected Fuller's belief that scientific progress could benefit everyone.

The geodesic dome was designed to serve several educational functions, says Kirk Bergstrom, president of media design firm WorldLink and former vice chair of the Buckminster Fuller Institute in San Francisco. "First, the structure represents a physical expression of Fuller's synergetic geometry, the coordinate system of nature... A dome embodies the principle of 'doing more with less,'" he says. "Second, the spherical framework can function as a 'geoscope'— one of Fuller's inventions to display global trends and patterns on the interior membrane of a

dome. Third, a dome represents a potential learning environment. Its arching, open architecture provides a flexible and modular space for design labs, group process, and artistic performance."

An inventor and philosopher, Fuller is remembered for his concept of Spaceship Earth as well as his visionary creations. He was influenced by the writing of self-improvement guru Alfred Korzybski, who was known for his adage that "the map is not the territory." Fuller was also an autodidact who was very at home preaching unconventional ideas. He popularized the geodesic dome as a kind of mass housing that could be transported by aircraft. His UFO-like Dymaxion homes were hung from masts and could be packed up and moved. Some of his Dymaxion car designs were flying vehicles that anticipated today's drone taxis. Though thousands of domes were

"Fuller felt that schools destroyed a child's intuitive grasp of the world."

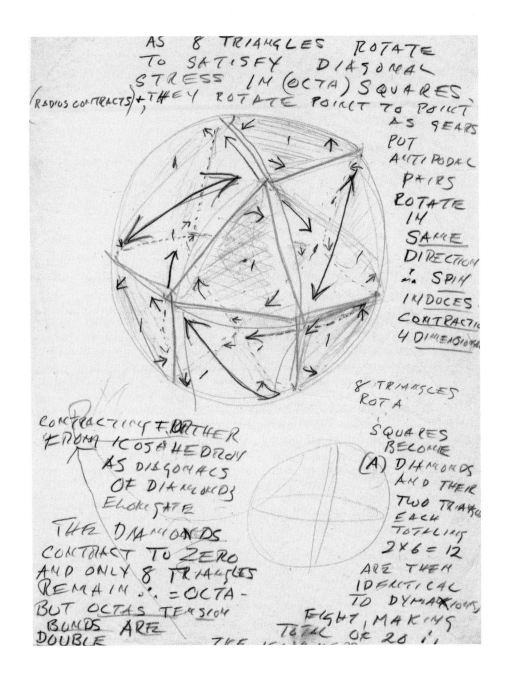

"What we had to do, he said, was be naive and follow nature's design principles."

built in the 1950s and '60s, neither his architecture nor his vehicles sparked the sea change in thinking that he longed for.

Fuller tried education reform, drawing inspiration from experience. Born in Massachusetts in 1895, he was not a promising child. Short and cross-eyed, he was bullied in school and argued with his teachers. He got into Harvard only to be kicked out twice. After a bout of depression and an attempted suicide, he committed himself to improving the lot of humanity.

Fuller felt that schools destroyed a child's intuitive grasp of the world by forcing knowledge into silos. "He found the goal of education was to 'de-genius' the child, for, as he said, 'every child is born a genius,'" Fuller's daughter Allegra Fuller Snyder explained in

a 1998 interview. Railing against schools was a favorite theme in Fuller's many lectures, which carried on for hours in great torrents of logorrhea. He conveyed his unshakable belief that pollution, overpopulation, inequality and the other global problems could be mitigated by education, science and technology. People responded with standing ovations.

One of these monologues became a 1962 book, *Education Automation: Comprehensive Learning for Emergent Humanity*. In it, he wrote, "What usually happens in the educational process is that the faculties are dulled, overloaded, stuffed and paralyzed, so that by the time that most people are mature they have lost use of many of their innate capabilities. My longtime hope is that we may soon

begin to realize what we are doing and may alter the 'education' process in such a way as only to help the new life to demonstrate some of its very powerful innate capabilities."

The book predicted that automation would make most work obsolete, and people would spend the majority of their time on reeducation to stay abreast of progress. Fuller foresaw the rise of lifelong education, massive online open courses (MOOCs), and even YouTube lessons and TED Talks. "The individual is going to study mainly at home," Fuller said in a 1966 interview in *The New Yorker*. "And the great teachers won't have to spend their time delivering the same lectures over and over, because they'll put them on film. The teachers and scholars will be

free to spend their time developing more and more knowledge about man's whole experience—past, present, and future."

"By exploring the world around him without preconceptions, Fuller believed that he could discover patterns that would lead to the reorganization of society in ways that would benefit everybody," says Jonathon Keats, author of *You Belong to the Universe: Buckminster Fuller and the Future*. "Of course he didn't succeed."

Fuller had little tolerance for independent thinking among his students, Keats adds, and sometimes viewed them as free labor for his projects. But he emphasized that curiosity should be the driver of education, an idea that resonates widely today. "His educational impact was probably most profound where he was least directly involved, where people went to his lectures (often stoned) and got the gist of his way of thinking without learning too many details—let alone coming under his direct instruction," says Keats. "For them, and for those who study Fuller today, I believe he can be inspiring in the best possible way."

In 1976, a fire broke out at the former American pavilion in Montreal, leaving the dome a charred skeleton. It later played the part of a ruined alien city in *Battlestar Galactica*, with an android gazing wistfully at the structure and lamenting, "It was beautiful... once upon a time." For years, the dome lay abandoned.

Fortunately, that wasn't the end of Fuller's greatest creation. More than a decade after his death in 1983, Environment Canada reopened the pavilion as a museum dedicated to the environment. Later renamed the Montreal Biosphere, it's the only facility of its kind in North America, and is dedicated to raising awareness about environmental issues. Today, the dome sparkles over the Saint Lawrence River, a monument to Spaceship Earth. Surely Bucky would be proud.

Designed in 1940, the Dymaxion Deployment Unit was a bombproof shelter inspired by the structure of a grain silo. Like many of Fuller's designs, it was intended to be portable.

EDUCATION

LI

LESSONS:

The B sides of education, learned at the school of life. Photography by Gustav Almestål & Set Design by Matilda Beckman

Fig. 1.

600 "

500 "

400 "

300 "

200 "

100 "

0

27 = 0,0

(Vitesse)

0,25

0,50

0,75

Tauchung
(Tirant d'eau)

400 kg

Nora McInerny explains why strangers' stories are the backbone of emotional learning.

Words:
Bella Gladman

1:

MIND

Nora McInerny stepped into the role of grief educator in 2015 after having a miscarriage and losing her father, and her husband, Aaron, in just a few months. An advertising copywriter, she had blogged through Aaron's cancer journey; as a couple, they co-wrote a moving yet hilarious obituary for him. Since his death, she has written two memoirs and a book of advice for grievers, founded a nonprofit and started hosting the wildly popular podcast *Terrible, Thanks for Asking.* The podcast is an extension of McInerny's belief that we can learn about ourselves through the stories of others—and an excuse for people to have a good cry on their commute, which, she says laughing, is the whole point.

BG: *Why is personal storytelling such an important part of educating people about dealing with difficult emotions?* **NM:** At first, I was learning a whole new way of being in the world [as a widow] and nobody around me had learned it yet either. It was a lonely place to be. I wanted to share my experience because I didn't have anything to read about going through grief in the moment—only books examining it from a great distance. They were helpful, of course, but being "in" something is just as valid a perspective. Once people heard my story, so many reached out with stories of their own, because they felt as alone as I had. I started the podcast to shift away from my story and into other people's, to create spaces for empathy. You can learn so much from stories that aren't exactly yours. You hear something and think, "I've felt like that."

BG: *How does your work fit in around existing self-help narratives?* **NM:** There's an oppressive form of internet optimism, where you must turn bad things into good,

and be a better version of yourself very quickly. Maybe that happens in time, but at first, it sucks! If I could rip out [societal expectations] at the roots, I would. That mentality says suffering is an error in our human experience, when it's not: It's part of the full experience. We can't rush ourselves or each other through that.

BG: *What advice do you have for people wanting to open up a painful conversation?* **NM:** When it comes down to it, humility is required, both for the person in pain to do their best to explain how it feels and admit, "I don't know what I need," and for the person supporting them to remove their ego, and be okay with somebody not responding the way you want them to.

BG: *What made you think that podcasting would be a good format for these conversations?* **NM:** I can't say it was strategic; one thing led to another. I wrote the first book [*It's Okay to Laugh (Crying Is Cool Too)*] and got so many responses—the podcast was the best way to reach the most people. I couldn't sit at my computer answering emails one by one through the night anymore. The podcast episodes give you something to point people toward. Therapists have told me they use the episodes for discussions with patients.

BG: *What are the biggest misconceptions that people have about grief?* **NM:** People vastly overestimate the power they have to ruin your day by bringing difficult topics up. But pretending they don't exist is impossible. I love learning things about Aaron and my dad's lives that I didn't know before. Also, thinking that I should be in a certain place with my grief made me miserable for a long time. My podcast producer Hans' grandma passed on this advice: "Don't let anyone 'should' on you, and don't you 'should' on yourself either."

Jessamyn Stanley is proud to be breaking the myth of yoga as a practice for "skinny, rich white women in expensive leggings." "If you can breathe, you can do this practice," she says. It seems quite basic, but judging from the reaction that this "fat femme" has caused throughout the international yoga community, you'd think she'd invented an entirely new form of exercise. Stanley, who lives in North Carolina, has become not just a yoga instructor but a body positivity advocate and an online educator.

DDJ: *What made you want to teach yoga?* **JS:** I do feel like I was called to do it. If you don't go into teaching yoga with the intention of making money, I think you are able to appreciate it in a different way. I'm always trying to hold space and make space for people to have the experiences they need to have. Often, it's hard for us to just get into our own bodies. We're so focused on what's going on around us. The only guide that I have for doing that work is just trying to do it for myself.

    DDJ: *How can we teach the next generation to love their bodies?* **JS:** The best way to teach children to love their bodies is to practice loving your own body. The most powerful influence on children is watching how adults act. If we're saying hateful things to one another, or if we're saying hateful things to ourselves, they know that they came from us and that we all are connected. So starting with yourself and fundamentally shifting that can have astronomical effects.

    DDJ: *As a black woman, what do you feel we need to learn about how the body is connected to politics?* **JS:** I think that everything is political. I think that we are all political. Pretending as though that's not the case is just omitting a huge aspect of the reason that we're all connecting with one another. I feel a responsibility to my lineage to really be in the truth of my own power and my political existence regardless of what that means for other people. No matter what the reaction is, it's always what's necessary.

    DDJ: *Is there something that you can share about how you unlearn the bad messages about your body?* **JS:** In my experience, the only thing that can really be done is to stop listening to the opinions of other people. It doesn't mean that you stop hearing them. It just means stop listening to them. Everyone wants to hear a "magic mantra": Something that I can say or buy, that's going to make me figure it all out. Capitalism is fully supported by us hating ourselves. But there's nothing to buy. If you want a mantra, I would say it's probably something like "I am." We can start with that.

    Individually, we can each make a difference in our immediate communities, which is really all that matters. I always think, "How can I work on myself and allow that to reflect to other people?" That will eventually create large, long-term, large-scale change in how we educate ourselves and others about our bodies—and our place on this planet.

Jessamyn Stanley is on a mission to smash the body hierarchy.

2:

BODY

Words:
Djassi DaCosta
Johnson

3:

SPIRIT

University chaplain *Khalid Latif* is teaching much more than the Quran.

Words:
John Clifford Burns

Khalid Latif was the first Muslim chaplain at New York University—a role he had previously undertaken for Princeton and the New York Police Department. He also serves as the executive director of the university's Islamic Center, where he teaches a course called "Multifaith Leadership in the 21st Century" alongside Rabbi Judah Sarna. It would be hard to find someone better qualified for the post than Latif: A pillar of his community, he owns a halal butcher shop, Honest Chops, is a father of two and managed to raise just short of one million dollars over the month of Ramadan for a domestic violence shelter in New York City. Here, he explains how he encourages students "to self-express, to feel comfortable in making their own decisions and to recognize that they don't have to let go of their religious identity in order to find a place of belonging."

JCB: *Your students spend their days occupied by "book learning." How is spiritual learning different?* **KL:** The era that we're in is quite anti-intellectual in that the training you have will give you the skills to be a doctor or a lawyer or an engineer or a scientist. But as you're learning to be a worker, who's really teaching you how to be a thinker?

JCB: *Where does the line between religious doctrine and spiritual guidance fall?* **KL:** Religion at times can be quite intimidating for many people, especially when you have organized, structured religion that functions off of a legalistic framework and has do's and don'ts, which translate in the minds of many as rights and wrongs. For many of the students that we see, religion has just been those mechanics. What we try to offer is an opportunity for them to affirm themselves. What really is their philosophy on life?

JCB: *What are some of the challenges facing students today?* **KL:** We see people across the board with every issue that you could imagine. To be young and Muslim right now in the United States is a very difficult experience. And New York City—more so than most places—necessitates that people are a facade of themselves at all times in order to be accepted and not show any sense of what would be perceived as weakness or struggle.

JCB: *How can the guidance you give to students impact the larger community?* **KL:** American society is built off of a very pervasive egocentricity. It puts the individual at the center of everything and many of us then believe that we are the center of everything, rather than thinking that there are many other spheres of engagement and interaction. When we expose ourselves to spaces that are distinct from our own, it creates an opportunity to learn quite differently. Stand with people to be able to deepen an understanding.

JCB: *How do you measure success in your role?* **KL:** We've gotten all kinds of awards and accolades and I've shared stages with people like Pope Francis and the Dalai Lama, but the affirmation to me is seeing somebody walk into my office and say, "Hey, you know what? I do want to go and build that domestic violence shelter. How do we make it happen?" They are recognizing their own potential and they're moving forward with it.

4:

NATURE

Words:
Neda Semnani

More than seven-hundred and fifty million years ago, an ocean covered the globe. Then, an ancient continent broke up. The waters receded. The story of this old ocean is embedded in the desert of southern Utah. The guides here talk about the world in increments of thousands, millions and billions of years. They point to tracks left by dinosaurs and the ancient petroglyphs sketched high on the rock face; the sedimentary layers of the rich, red Navajo Sandstone formations and the blackened lava fields speak to a time long before that.

It is as if everything here has always existed this way in this place, and yet rooted in the cliffs and desert sands is a story of constancy, of change and of resilience. "This was the bottom of the ocean," one guide explains, her gesture taking in the ground and the rock face around her. "What's left of that ocean is the Great Salt Lake," another guide says.

Today, as the climate changes quickly and dramatically because of human interventions, people are experiencing solastalgia, or distress and trauma from seeing, learning about and experiencing the dire implications of the Earth's changing climate. Daily there are images of homes burning, flooding, sinking and blowing away. Helplessness and hopelessness are pervasive. In a report released in 2017 by the American Psychological Association, Climate for Health and ecoAmerica, it is clear that climate change affects the psyche. There are acute and chronic mental health implications: anxiety disorders, depression, post-traumatic stress disorder, anti-social behaviors, drug abuse and even suicide.

"When the sorrow and grief do come up, I encourage clients to feel what they are feeling," says Sumitra Rajkumar, a Brooklyn-based somatic therapist, "I tell them it makes sense." The treatment for this existential grief, in part, is deceptively simple. "The strange gift of grief is that relationships become more valuable and worth fighting for," says Rajkumar. So, be more active and eco-aware of what is happening and how to help. Be in nature as often as possible. And work to strengthen individual and communal resilience.

Resiliency, after all, is a skill, and it can be learned from the stories of our ever-evolving, always-healing Earth. She has the wisdom of billions and billions of years; we're still new here.

Words:
Pip Usher

For new parents, there's no shortage of how-to manuals that tackle everything from sleep training to tantrums. But life hacks aside, how exactly does one take a tiny baby and turn them into an emotionally healthy adult?

Your greatest chance for success, argues psychotherapist Philippa Perry, is to understand yourself first. In her bestselling guide to parenthood, *The Book You Wish Your Parents Had Read (and Your Children Will Be Glad That You Did)*, Perry urges parents to understand their "parenting legacy"—that singular narrative of the childhood experiences that have shaped each one of us into the adult we are today. Perry believes that a thorough understanding of one's own history equips parents to identify—and then avoid—the unhelpful habits that were taught to them as children. "We are but a link in a chain stretching back through millennia and forwards until who knows when," she writes. "The good news is that you can learn to reshape your link, and this will improve the life of your children, and their children, and you can start now."

Imagine that you're sorting through your childhood home. As you gaze around a bedroom cluttered with belongings, some will be treasured souvenirs that elicit warm memories. Those will be packed up and brought to your new home, where they can continue to contribute to the happiness of your family. Other items might provoke memories of fear, loneliness or shame. These are better left behind.

When it comes to soul-searching, it's a similar process. Unpack the past, examine how you feel about it and then take only what's worth passing on to your own children. "We cannot put anything right if we feel too ashamed to admit to our faults," Perry advises.

Often, this self-examination will give new meaning to the negative emotions that your child stirs up in you. Should you find yourself responding with hostility when they make boisterous bids for your attention, there's probably a reason that can be traced back to your early relationships. Once that trigger is understood, it becomes easier to empathize with your child and understand their needs separately from your own internal narrative.

A quick fix it is not—although as Perry cheerfully points out, childrearing isn't supposed to be easy. It's a messy, unpredictable marathon with no guarantees. There will be hurt feelings, hot tempers and a whole bunch of mistakes made along the way. Take the time to reflect on these mishaps. You'll be surprised by what you find.

5: PARENT —ING

Before you try and teach your children, learn about your past.

At Work With:
Liz Kleinrock

How should children be taught about consent, homelessness and the meaning of "microaggression"?
Robert Ito meets *Liz Kleinrock* as she prepares for her final term as an elementary school teacher, before setting off on a mission to improve diversity and anti-bias training nationwide. Photography by *Emman Montalvan* & Styling by *Patricia Lagmay*

Page 164: Kleinrock wears a top by Une Heures, a skirt by Mijeong Park and sandals by COS. Page 165: She wears a sweater and sweater dress by Pari Desai and trousers by Shaina Mote. Left (and overleaf): She wears a dress by Nanushka. Below: She wears a dress by LVIR and a turtleneck by Nanushka.

For the past eight years, Liz Kleinrock, a grade school teacher in Los Angeles, has discussed all manner of topics with her students. Conversations range from the serious (the homelessness crisis) to the whimsical ("If you woke up tomorrow as a 30-year-old, what would you do?"). In 2017, she began posting some of her favorite classroom discussions on Instagram, in the hopes of sharing and connecting with other like-minded teachers. "When I got my first 10 followers who didn't know me, I was like, 'Oh, this is really cool!'" she says, speaking at a coffee shop in Larchmont Village. "I'm meeting people."

But when Kleinrock shared a lesson plan on consent—what it means, why we need to ask for it—the post quickly went viral. Soon, newcomers to her page were discovering older posts about everything from food deserts and housing discrimination to how to pump yourself up when you're feeling down. Since then, Kleinrock, who was born in South Korea and raised in Washington, D.C., has received a teaching award from Teaching Tolerance, an offshoot of the Southern Poverty Law Center, delivered a TED Talk entitled "How to Teach Kids to Talk About Taboo Topics" and signed a book deal—which she's taking time out from teaching to work on. Still, she remains humble about the post that, in many ways, started it all. "These are conversations that most teachers in elementary school are having with their kids anyway," she says. "Don't put your hands on people. Ask with your words, not with your hands. I was just giving them the adult vocabulary to go with it."

RI: *You spend a lot of time with kids. What were you like growing up?* **LK:** My kindergarten teacher wrote a comment about how I was the kid who didn't want to come to the circle when it was circle time. I believe her quote was "Elizabeth can be found sitting in a corner reading or talking to herself." I read a lot.

RI: *Were you a good student?* **LK:** Academically, I was pretty average, if not below average. I went to Sidwell Friends in D.C., which is a really elite private school. It's where the Obama girls went. Chelsea Clinton went there. I think I spent most of my childhood just feeling like I wasn't as smart as the person sitting next to me.

RI: *Did those experiences affect how you approach your own students?* **LK:** It's really helped me think about how I discuss and define success in the classroom. I want my students to feel recognized for what they can bring to the table, instead of being defined by what they can't do (which, unfortunately, is how things tend to go in public education). We label students as "English language learners" instead of praising them for being emerging bilingual students. I would love to be completely fluent in another language!

Spanish

Music

Readers Workshop

Recess

Lunch

Read Aloud

T.F.U.

"Everybody has biases—kids have biases—but they're not as jaded as adults."

RI: *Did you have a sense early on that things were not fair in the world?* **LK:** I think if you ask my parents they would probably say yes. My school emphasized philanthropy at a young age. I remember being exposed to reminders of how privileged I was very early and not really understanding why everybody couldn't have access to what they needed. It's something that I love about working with young kids. All little kids are really just socialists. They want to give everything to everybody.

RI: *Tell me about how your consent lesson came about.* **LK:** I was watching some truly heartbreaking testimony of a woman reliving her trauma from her youth, and watching the general public skewer her. And it wasn't just that one incident, it was every article that highlighted a case of sexual assault or abuse on college campuses or in the workplace, and just thinking that this is a cycle that's never going to stop unless we get to people early. I wondered what those people who committed those acts were told as kids, or if they were ever introduced to the concept of boundaries. What kind of foundation can we lay down for kids so they grow up to be better? I feel like that's the basis for all of this work. How can we make kids better than us?

RI: *What was it like when the post went viral?* **LK:** Really exciting and great for two or three days. And then overwhelming, and I wanted it all to go away.

RI: *Were there things you had to learn the hard way about social media?* **LK:** You can't please everybody, and it's unrealistic to think that you can. I got a lot of hate mail. I went out for Peking duck with my family after my TED Talk in New York, and I posted a celebratory picture on my Instagram story, and someone responded, "It's really disappointing and irresponsible that you would be using your platform to promote eating meat." I've had people criticize the food that I feed my bunny.

RI: *And yet are there a lot of positives, too?* **LK:** I think so. It has already started to connect teachers who feel isolated and disconnected. There are some really cool conferences that take place online, so teachers from all over the country can attend virtually. And there's the community part,

too. I know that there are teachers out there who I talk to more frequently than I talk to some of my really close friends. There are teachers I have met through Instagram who are real-life friends, which is awesome.

RI: *When I was teaching at UCLA, a lot of my undergrad students hadn't really thought about many of the topics you discuss with your third and fourth grade kids. What do you tell people who say that grade schoolers are too young to be talking about these issues?* **LK:** More often than not, the unwillingness to engage kids in these kinds of conversations comes from adults not knowing how to navigate those topics themselves. And they assume that if they can't as adults, then therefore kids probably can't either. But I find it to be completely the opposite. Everybody has biases—kids have biases—but they're not as jaded as adults. And when they get the inkling that somebody's inviting them into a conversation about a topic that's usually reserved for grownups, they just get so much more excited about it.

RI: *You've also done a lot of work on racial issues in your classroom. When did you first become conscious of race?* **LK:** I can't remember ever not being conscious of it. I knew that the yellow Power Ranger on TV was the only character who looked like me, and therefore whenever we played games outside, that's who I wanted to be. There was one Korean boy in my class, and I remember in kindergarten or first grade, somehow being convinced that, "Oh, I have to marry him, because he's the only one who looks like me."

RI: *In a perfect world, what would schools look like, and how would kids move through them?* **LK:** In a perfect world, schools would be much more student-centered. I think a lot of schools say that they're student-centered, but they're really not. In a perfect world, teachers are the facilitators in the classroom, but the students are the leaders. I would love to see students out of the classroom, or out of school more often, going into their communities to learn about what people are doing, or building or creating. And I want their curiosity to be honored. I think a lot of teachers view the kid who's always asking "Why this?" "Why that?" as a hindrance. I love my kids who are always asking why.

SPOT THE

DIFFER ENCE

Train your brain with these Spot the Difference and Odd One Out picture riddles.

Photography by *Aaron Tilley* & Styling by *Lisa Jahovic*

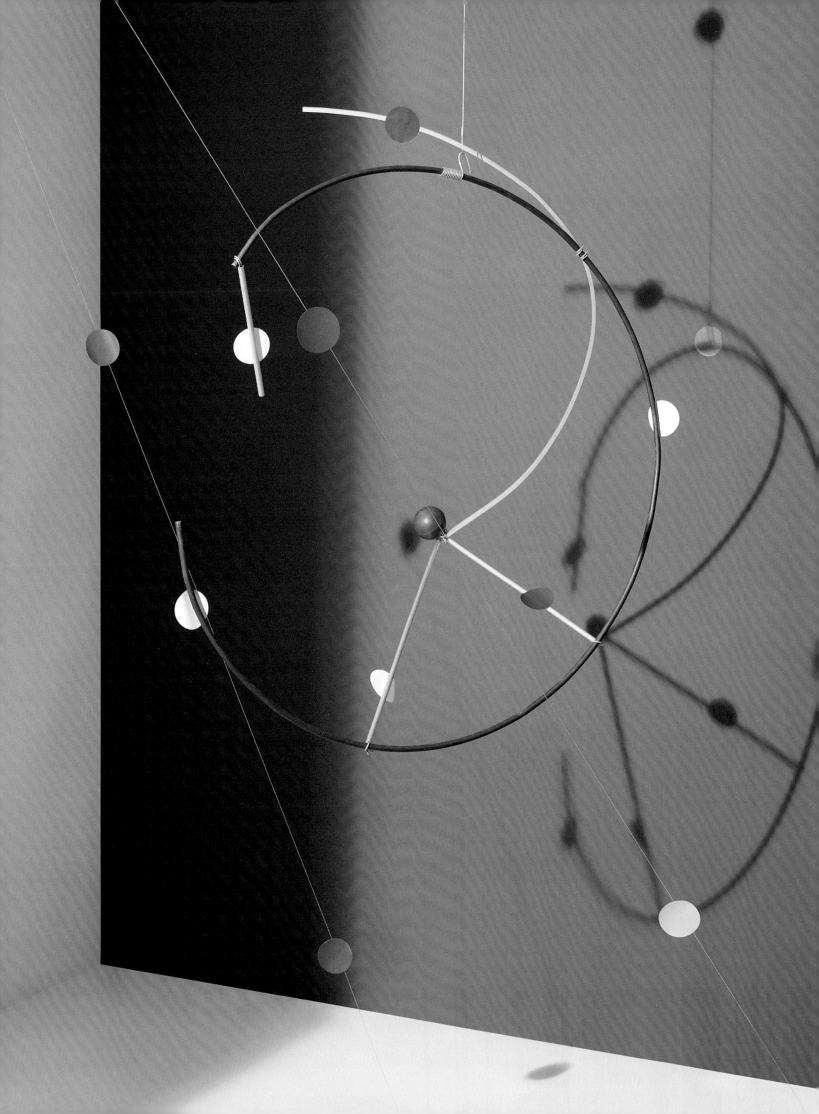

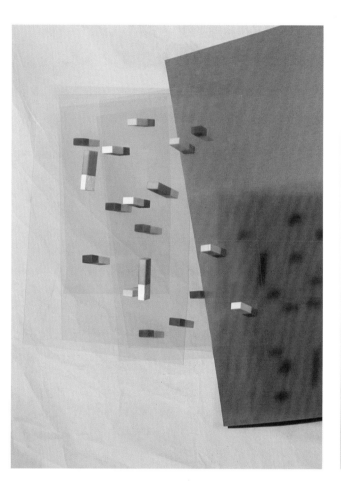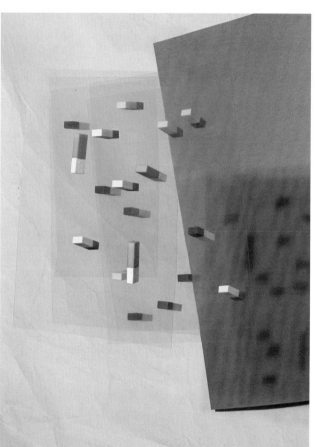

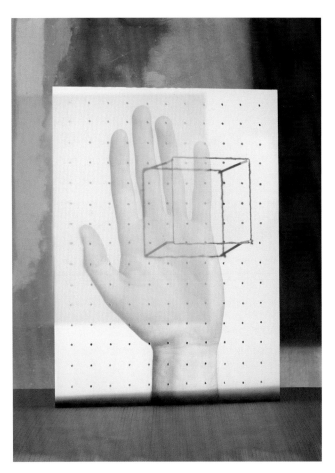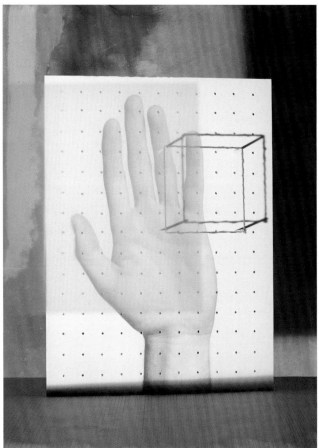

4
Directory

STEPHANIE D'ARC TAYLOR

Cult Rooms

Black Mountain College was an incubator for visionary designers, but the campus itself was a hodgepodge of styles—and a health and safety nightmare.

As is often the case with bright-burning ideas, the lore surrounding Black Mountain College looms much larger than the project itself. The hype is understandable: Over the course of just 24 years, in a hamlet in rural North Carolina, the college established itself as an inflection point in the trajectory of 20th-century art and education. Founded in 1933, the school was the ideological heir of Germany's famed Bauhaus school, and provided refuge and employment for artists and scholars fleeing rising fascism in Europe. Many of the students who attended the college would go on to comprise the vanguard of the avant-garde in the 1950s, '60s, and beyond; these included Cy Twombly, Merce Cunningham, John Cage and Allen Ginsberg.

Admirers may have assumed that Black Mountain College—the stomping ground of visionary architects and designers like Bauhaus pioneers Walter Gropius and Josef and Anni Albers—was architecturally interesting. It was, but not because any one building was exceptionally beautiful or groundbreaking. In fact, the architecture of the college was mismatched and unprofessionally built, says Alice Sebrell, Program Director of the Black Mountain College Museum + Arts Center, based in the nearby town of Asheville, North Carolina.

From its inaugural semester in the fall of 1933, Black Mountain College operated out of rented YMCA buildings. College life was centered around Robert E. Lee Hall, a three-story plantation-style mansion converted to dormitories, with a large lobby for lectures,

concerts and meetings. In 1939, faced with eviction, the college commissioned Gropius and his collaborator Marcel Breuer to design a new, purpose-built campus on the shores of nearby Lake Eden, incorporating input from the community. Endless deliberation—the college was founded with the idealistic goal of consensus-based decision-making—turned into fundraising problems. With the eviction deadline looming, the college asked A. Lawrence Kocher, longtime editor of *Architectural Record* and champion of modern architecture, to draw up simpler, cheaper plans.

Kocher may have been a visionary, but he was also a practical man. While Gropius and Breuer wanted to tear existing buildings down and start from scratch, he proposed to repurpose buildings on the property that had been part of a girls' camp and family resort, including a dining hall, a roundhouse to be used for concerts and music instruction and cottages to house married faculty and students. These buildings had been constructed in an "Appalachian vernacular style," says Sebrell. "Stone and mortar walls, wooden beams; the houses were built using materials that were probably gathered around this area."

Of course, Kocher's plans also included modern designs based on needs communicated by the college's Board of Fellows. His Studies Building included private offices for every student and faculty member. Its design couldn't be more different from the folksy lodge architecture of the other buildings on the lake. "It's a long,

Photograph: The Studies Building and
Lake Eden, Black Mountain College
by Harriet Sohmers Zwerling, 1949.
Courtesy of the Black Mountain College
Museum + Arts Center.

horizontal building with a flat roof that looks very minimal," Sebrell says. "The exterior material is a corrugated material called transite; it was affordable and came in sheets which would be hung." Panels of windows reflected the water from the lake, which was much closer at the time of construction than it is now.

The building projects incubated the college's architecture and product design programs. Students and faculty alike helped with the construction of the Studies Building; students were tasked with completing their private offices, down to designing and building the furniture. Sometimes their inexperience shows in the results, says Sebrell: "The stonework in the Studies Building definitely reflects a variation in skill level." A student-designed and constructed science center was so precarious that instructor Natasha Goldowski refused to set foot in the building after it was constructed in the early 1950s. Classes were held instead in the cavernous Studies Building.

The architectural jumble at Black Mountain College reflected its experimental, sometimes chaotic nature, an organic outgrowth of the founders' ethos of collaborative and multidisciplinary learning. Radically, the college posited art-making as the keystone of a progressive education. To the founders, the practice of creating art would develop skills including critical thinking, problem solving and collaboration, resulting in well-rounded young people prepared for life, not simply a career.

BEN SHATTUCK

Elizabeth Strout

Bestselling author Elizabeth Strout grew up on a dirt road in Brunswick, Maine—a town with a population of only 15,000 at the time. Composed of rocky peninsulas streaking into the sea, Brunswick would become the fertile ground for so many of Strout's most beloved stories. After moving to New York City, her writing returned to small-town Maine, culminating in her most famous novel, *Olive Kitteridge*, which won the 2009 Pulitzer Prize for Fiction. Her seventh novel, *Olive, Again*, will be published in October. She now splits her time between New York City and Maine.

BS: *You often use the word "truth" when talking about your work. Why is truth so important in your writing, given that you're a novelist?* **ES:** I came across this famous Hemingway quote many years ago: "All a writer needs to do is get up and write the most truthful sentence they know." It always stayed in my head. For years, I kept thinking, "I'm trying to write a truthful sentence," but I intuitively understood that I wasn't. I was writing the way I thought a writer should write. I finally figured it out: Just saying it as directly as one can, peeling away all the worries of judgment. Everybody, I think, has some kernel of truth, though they may not say it to many people. I write from that. Only that truth will reflect itself in the way the sentence sounds.

BS: *You're so adept at observing reality and putting it down on paper. Do you think you were born with that ability, or did you learn it?* **ES:** I must have been born with some ability, but I've also trained myself to acquire it over the years. It's just discipline. Rereading what I've written again and again, recognizing it's not right—usually because it's soggy. So pare it back, and pare it back, and pare it back until it's truthful.

BS: *Do you feel like you've gained a sharper perspective about your work or life as you've matured as a writer?* **ES:** As I get older, I have a much hazier sense of anything that would be called a higher consciousness, and yet I'm not opposed to any of those things. There are things that I write sometimes, and then they come true. That's a little bizarre. I think, "Well, maybe I'm shuffling between universes."

BS: *As a child, you had a strong relationship with nature. After living in the city for so much of your life, do you still seek that connection to nature?* **ES:** You know, I don't. I think that it was only available to me because I was so young, and it was the first thing I knew. I hadn't seen any big buildings, and I was very isolated. I was by myself with the beautiful world around me. I don't experience that anymore. I do mourn the loss a little bit, but not too deeply. There are times when I'm on the top of this building that I live in in New York, and I see the whole city, and it's just breathtaking in a whole different way. I realize, "Oh my word, look at everything. This is amazing what we've done." It's a little bit of a similar feeling, but it only lasts briefly.

BS: *You've said that after you moved to New York you didn't find success in writing for a long time— where did the drive to keep writing come from?* **ES:** From the ultimate desire to express myself to somebody else. When I was writing *Amy & Isabelle*, I used to hope fervently that just one or two people would read that book. I always wanted a particular kind of person to please, please find this book, and please may it mean something to you. The desire to communicate from my mind to the mind of another person is always there.

Although Strout always wanted to be a writer, she published her first novel at 42. She was 52 when she won the Pulitzer Prize for *Olive Kitteridge*.

New Tricks

Deciphering the limits of extreme animal grooming.

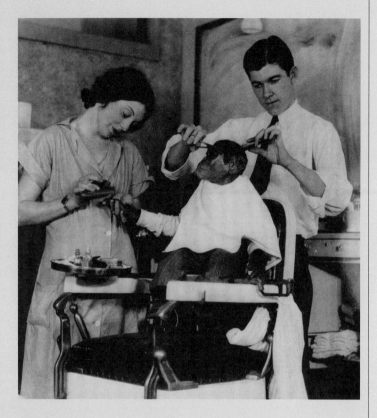

Dogs have come a long way. Their evolution from wolves took centuries, whereas today they can be made to look like robots, kangaroos, crustaceans and mermaids by extreme animal groomers in one sitting. It's not just dogs—around the world chicks and rabbits are dyed Crayola-bright in time for Easter, and cats' fur is buzzed to resemble flowers.

The artistry is laudable, but the ethics are questionable. Animal rights charities argue that pets are being anthropomorphized in unsettling new ways: People see them as an alternative to children and, without new shoes and school books to buy, there's cash available for multicolored makeovers. Some animal lovers worry that in addition to experiencing physical discomfort, pets are also being humiliated. "We are not greatly in favor of doing anything to dogs that makes them feel 'silly,'" Caroline Kisko, secretary of Britain's Kennel Club, told The Times of London in 2017. "Dogs know when they are being laughed at." Humiliation seems like a very human emotion to attribute to a dog. Indeed, humans have found so many ways to anthropomorphize domestic animals that the question

of what exactly "nature" means is not always obvious. Lines can feel a little blurred: Having a dog on a leash is expected, but where do we stand on carrying a dog in a handbag? Owners have shifted animals' habits, appearance and even DNA so drastically that in many ways they have become more of an extension of the human world than of the wild one. Over the course of thousands of years, animals have become domesticated—a process defined as the adaptation of animals for human use—for work, clothing, medicine, food and companionship. From sheep to goats, horses to the Syrian golden hamster—domesticated in 1930 and now spinning in wheels across the world—we've used animals for many things; perhaps humor is just the next frontier.

This need to "civilize" nature is present far beyond the world of pets; it's expressed in everything from manicured parks to privet hedges pruned to resemble teapots. But with talk of rewilding nature ever louder, maybe we should look close to home and let our pets express the last remnants of their wild side. Transforming animals into the butt of a very human joke seems like a ruff deal.

ON THE CATWALK
by Pip Usher

From the ancient Egyptians' fondness for draping their cats in jewels to the caviar-fueled existence of Karl Lagerfeld's beloved feline, Choupette, animals have long provided an outlet for human aspiration and self-aggrandizement. If clothes maketh the man, then perhaps designer goods maketh the man's dog—an idea recently capitalized upon by luxury brands that are branching out into pet accessory lines. Are pets grateful for Ralph Lauren's canine-sized cashmere sweaters or woven leather collars by Bottega Veneta? Probably not—but that was never really the point in the first place. (Top: Leash by Maxim Customs. Center: Saddle Oil by Hermès. Bottom: Rope Tug by Mungo & Maud.)

Right Photograph: Photography: FPG / Getty Images, Left Photographs: Photography: Courtesy of Maxim Customs, Hermès and Mungo & Maud

Quick tips for a good disguise.

Photograph: Edward Steichen / Condé Nast / Getty Images

PIP USHER

How to Disappear

When communist militant Cesare Battisti was arrested after decades on the run, he was employing the oldest trick in the criminal handbook: a disguise. Normally clean-shaven, the Italian fugitive was sporting a fake beard. Prior to his capture, the police had released images that illustrated 20 other possible disguises he might have adopted, from thick-rimmed glasses to a shaved head.

It may sound like a scene straight from a screwball comedy, but research has revealed the surprising effectiveness of appearance-altering ruses as a way to conceal one's identity. Dr. Rob Jenkins, a psychologist at the University of York, recently carried out a study that distinguished between two types of disguise available: evasion and impersonation. The former's goal is to no longer look like yourself, as favored by criminals, undercover cops and those in witness protection programs. The latter's aim is to imitate another person in order to pass yourself off as them. "When it comes to changing appearance, an important question is, 'To what end?'" Jenkins wrote in his study.

After recruiting models for the study, Jenkins asked them to change their appearance as much as possible, with a cash prize for the disguise that fooled the most people. Hair was dyed, facial hair grown and heavy makeup applied.

When participants were then shown two photographs and asked to judge whether it was the same or different people in them, their ability to accurately tell was reduced by around 30 percent. The research found that these evasion disguises were much more effective than those geared towards impersonation: Trying to look like *anyone* else is easier than mimicking a specific target.

But not all disguises require the time and effort that Jenkins' participants put in. In 2008, Todd Letcher, the head of the FBI's surveillance team in New York, gave an interview to NPR in which he explained that there's a far easier way to go incognito: Those wanting to go unnoticed simply need to look as commonplace as possible in order to blend into the background.

In dark shades and nondescript clothes, the fugitive Battisti certainly fit that bill. Could he have done a better job? Jenkins' research showed that fooling those familiar with your face requires intensive effort that can be difficult to sustain. "When you 'know' a face you tend to rely more on internal facial features—the eyes, nose and mouth—which are much harder to alter," he wrote. For Battisti, with his pronounced nose, it turned out a fake beard wasn't enough; Interpol had been pouring over his features since 1981.

Photograph: Portrait of Roland Barthes, 1979. © François Lagarde / Opale / Bridgeman Images

BLYTHE ROBERSON

Peer Review

Blythe Roberson, author of *How to Date Men When You Hate Men,* writes about *Roland Barthes.*

I don't know how I can recommend Roland Barthes any more highly than to say that my own book is based on Barthes' *A Lover's Discourse*—other than to say that I often loan *A Lover's Discourse* to hot men, as a flirt.

Reading the book for the first time felt like a friend flicking me in the head over and over going, "Duh, duh, duh, duh, duh." Barthes breaks down the experience of being a lover into minute slices, unearthing the type of wriggly thoughts I had experienced but had never seen written about. The kind of thing like: "Are not excess and madness my truth, my strength?" And: "I lived in the complication of supposing myself simultaneously loved and abandoned"—huge for someone who has been single for stretches of time bordering on infinity, but who concurrently believes everyone to be secretly in love with her. I knew vaguely of Barthes before

I read *A Lover's Discourse,* but only in his capacity as a semiotician. (I have a four-year degree in English and all I can tell you about semiotics is that someone tried to explain it to me in college.) Barthes was a gay French literary theorist and philosopher. He was born in 1915 and died in 1980 and published *A Lover's Discourse* toward the end, in 1977. I'm pretty sure almost everything else he wrote is considered more serious, but I don't care. *A Lover's Discourse* alone makes Barthes, for me, an immortal hero.

Every cool person in the world loves this book, I've discovered. I watched Claire Denis' *Let The Sunshine In,* starring Juliette Binoche as a single woman in Paris. It was beautiful, funny, and made me seriously consider giving up trying to be sane in an "I'm friends with all my exes" way and instead, like Binoche's character, just start crying all the time. I googled the film: It's based on *A Lover's Discourse.*

CARRIED AWAY

by Harriet Fitch Little

When Gerry Cunningham first added zippers to a backpack design in the 1930s, he envisaged them as practical additions to bags for climbers such as himself. It's hard to imagine now that it wasn't until the 1970s—when they were offered for sale at the sports shop attached to the University of Washington bookstore—that students cottoned on that carrying books on their back might be more ergonomic than carrying them by hand or in a shoulder satchel. What was once a practical solution has, with time, become its own burden: Schoolbags are so big that chiropractors complain they're condemning a generation to chronic back pain. (Top: Tote Backpack by COS. Center: Drawstring Backpack by Balenciaga. Bottom: Mini Rucksack by Building Block.)

KATIE CALAUTTI

Object Matters

A zip through history.

It took almost 100 years after the introduction of the zipper for the contraption's capabilities and primary purpose to mesh.

Perhaps early zippers suffered from poor branding: Neither the Automatic, Continuous Clothing Closure created by Elias Howe in 1851, nor the Clasp Locker or Unlocker for Shoes unveiled at the 1893 Chicago World's Fair had quite the same catchy ring about them as the onomatopoeic "zipper." They were also poorly designed—early iterations tore clothing fabric and popped open at inopportune times.

The design of the zipper as we know it came about in the early 1900s, but was still shunned by society as a fleeting curiosity that promoted a swift state of undress. It was relegated to fastening tobacco pouches and money belts for World War I sailors, whose uniforms didn't have pockets.

It was in the 1930s that savvy salespeople managed to convince the public that zippers could be useful—and perhaps even fashionable. Ads for children's clothing touted outfits bearing zippers as promoting self-reliance in youngsters, and haute couture designer Elsa Schiaparelli set her 1935 collection apart by incorporating the device. But the zipper finally had its moment in the spotlight in 1937 when, following rave reviews from French fashion designers, it beat the button in *Esquire* magazine's "Battle of the Fly." Zippers soon replaced button flies in upscale men's trousers, becoming more standard in ready-to-wear items by the 1940s. Womenswear followed, and by the 1950s the zipper was the default fastener on most clothing. Hollywood caught on that decade, as well, using the zipper as a sign of rebellion via leather jackets: Through the 1970s, the zipper symbolized impulsiveness and unbridled sexuality. Over the years, improvements kept being made. Whether they're waterproof, airtight or rust-proof, zippers are used everywhere from runways to NASA spacesuits. Now a $13 billion industry, the market is dominated by the Japanese YKK Group, which makes about half of all the zippers in the world. If you're looking for proof, just look down at the clasps on your clothing.

ANNA GUNDLACH

Crossword

Fill in the circled letters to learn where great minds are made.

THE LAST WORD

Imitation may be the sincerest form of flattery, but that doesn't make it any less irritating to see a prized personal project ripped off by someone else. Elementary schoolteacher *Liz Kleinrock*, interviewed on page 164, is well-versed in resolving spats about intellectual property—albeit among eight-year-olds. To close the Education Issue, she shares some tips from her class on giving credit where it's due.

My students all know that copying someone's work outright isn't okay, but they have mixed feelings about someone copying their clothing style or being inspired by an art project. It seems to depend a lot on who is copying them. If it's someone they're close to, they don't mind as much. (Although, across the board, they hate it when their siblings copy.) They also think that giving credit is important—some tell me that they don't mind being copied as long as the person didn't pretend that it was their idea all along. As an educator, I agree with them on that one. When I create content on race and equity for the classroom, I think it's great when other teachers replicate these lessons with their kids, but it has bothered me when some portray the lessons and activities as their original idea. When you put emotional and time-consuming labor into your work, it's okay to want to be credited for it. These days, I've noticed there's a lot that comes up around appropriation versus appreciation —in the creative industries, and in the classroom. A few years ago, my school was supposed to put on a play in which students were asked to portray Native Americans and black enslaved people. A group of teachers and parents felt that this was cultural appropriation (and also in poor taste) because the students were not properly educated about the histories, cultures and traditions. While all artists seek and acquire inspiration from the world around them, it feels disrespectful to "borrow" from other cultures without seeking to educate yourself, especially if you are gaining something financially or professionally from the work.

Stockists

A.P.C.
apc.fr

ADIDAS
adidas.com

AMI
amiparis.com

ANDREW SZEWCZYK
andrewszewczyk.com

ANNETTE FERDINANDSEN
annetteferdinandsen.com

BALMAIN
balmain.com

BASSIKE
bassike.com

BUILDING BLOCK
building--block.com

BULY 1803
buly1803.com

BYREDO
byredo.com

CHANEL
chanel.com

CHARVET
charvet.com

CLAUS PORTO
clausporto.com

COS
cosstores.com

DE FURSAC
defursac.fr

DIOR
dior.com

ELHANATI
elhanati.com

EMPORIO ARMANI
armani.com

ERIC BOMPARD
eric-bompard.com

FALKE
falke.com

FIFI CHACHNIL
fifichachnil.paris

GOLLNEST & KIESEL
gokishop.eu

HEM
hem.com

HERBIVORE BOTANICALS
herbivorebotanicals.com

HERMÈS
hermes.com

HOLIDAY BOILEAU
holiday-paris.fr

HUGO BOSS
hugoboss.com

J. M. WESTON
jmweston.com

KLEMENS SCHILLINGER
klemensschillinger.com

LVIR
lvir.us

LYNNE WEARE
lynneweare.com

LYST
lyst.com

MADIYAH AL SHARQI
madiyahalsharqi.com

MAXIM CUSTOMS
maximcustoms.com

MIJEONG PARK
mijeongpark.com

MR PORTER
mrporter.com

MR SMITH
mr-smith.com.au

NANUSHKA
nanushka.com

NOGUCHI
noguchi-bijoux.com

OCTOBRE EDITIONS
octobre-editions.com

OFF-WHITE
off-white.com

ORMAIE
ormaie.paris.com

PARI DESAI
paridesai.com

PAUL SMITH
paulsmith.com

PAUSTIAN
paustian.com

RACHEL COMEY
rachelcomey.com

REPETTO
repetto.com

ROCHAS
rochas.com

SACAI
sacai.jp

SANDRO
sandro-paris.com

SHAINA MOTE
shainamote.com

SILVIA TCHERASSI
silviatcherassi.com

SOPHIE BILLE BRAHE
sophiebillebrahe.com

THE ROW
therow.com

TODD SNYDER
toddsnyder.com

UNE HEURES
uneheures.com

VALENTINO
valentino.com

VINCENZO DE COTIIS
decotiis.it

VITRA
vitra.com

VIVIENNE WESTWOOD
viviennewestwood.com

WOLF&RITA

ISSUE 33

Credits

COVER
Photographer
Romain Laprade
Styling
Camille-Joséphine Teisseire
Hair & Makeup
Josephine Mai
Model
Wilbert Eskildsen at 2pm
Location
Nørre Vium Sports- Og
Kulturcenter

Wilbert wears a polo shirt by
De Fursac, vintage Adidas
shorts, a cap by Holiday
Boileau, socks by Falke and
sneakers by AMI.

P. 66 – 75
Photo Assistant
Jonas Bjurman
Models
Shalini Kellinghaus at MIKAs
Ivy Henriksson at MIKAs

P. 94 – 103
Hair
Taan Doan
Makeup
Cyril Laine
Models
Nataliya Bulycheva at
Elite Paris
Katya Bybina at Elite Paris
Victorien Blagonja at
Elite Paris
Anis Ben Choug at Elite Paris

Location
Chez Georges, Paris
Production
Nicolas Martin, Western
Promises
Dancers and Musicians
Ryan Ben Yaiche
Max Dindinaud
Clement Faure
Natasha Ouimet
Justine Roussillon
Fanny Sage
Patrick Sznidt

P. 104 – 105
Photography: *Thomas D.
Mcavoy*/The LIFE Picture
Collection/Getty Images

P. 114 – 123
Photo Assistants
Austin Calvello
Gray Hamner

P. 124 – 137
Model
Wilbert Eskildsen at 2pm
Location
Nørre Vium Sports- Og
Kulturcenter

Special Thanks:
Deborah Bell
Chez Georges
Citizens of the World
Charter School Silver Lake
Jelmar Hufen of H. Gallery
Shelby Hartness